The Black History Truth: JAMAICA

The Sharpest Thorn in Britain's Caribbean Colonies

Pamela Gayle

Grosvenor House
Publishing Limited

This book is published by
Grosvenor House Publishing Ltd
Link House
140 The Broadway, Tolworth, Surrey, KT6 7HT.
www.grosvenorhousepublishing.co.uk

A CIP record for this book
is available from the British Library

ISBN 978-1-80381-016-4
eBook ISBN 978-1-80381-089-8

Image 1: © The Sankofa symbol represents the importance of learning from the past. Adinkra Akan art symbol from Ghana.

Excerpts reproduced with kind permission from:

Abbreviations:

JIS	Jamaica Information Service
JEPA	Jamaica Environmental Protection Agency
JJ	Jamaica Journal
JNHT	Jamaican National Heritage Trust
NHM	National History Museum, London, UK
(n.d.)	no date
NLJ	National Library of Jamaica
UNESCO	United Nations Educational, Scientific and Cultural Organisation
UWI	University of the West Indies

5-STAR REVIEWS:

Reviewed by Astrid Lustulin for Readers' Favourite:
It is time to learn the stories of some nations in a more equitable way - not from the point of view of the conquerors but of the oppressed. This is why books like The Black History Truth: Jamaica by Pamela Gayle arouse great interest in a conscious reader. This book tells the story of 'The Sharpest Thorn in Britain's Caribbean Colonies,' focusing on the 16th to 19th centuries. Through extensive use of sources and images, Gayle sheds light on the injustices perpetrated by the British and analyses the stigmatization of Eurocentric historiography, which portrayed unfavorably behaviors and customs of groups of people it could not understand.

Although the subject is complex, this book is clear and precise. Gayle tackles so many topics that she arouses the admiration of readers with her profound knowledge of Jamaica. She is very direct when she blames the British, but the evidence she brings is overwhelming. In The Black History Truth: Jamaica, you will not only find descriptions of struggles and injustices but also valuable information on local heroes and heroines, such as Nana Yaa Asantewaa and Queen Nanny, as well as customs that Europeans have misunderstood. After reading this book, readers will understand why Jamaica was actually (as the subtitle describes it) "the sharpest thorn in Britain's Caribbean Colonies." I recommend this book to all those who want to see the history of humanity from a new perspective.

Reviewed by Sheena Monnin for Readers' Favourite:
The Black History Truth: Jamaica by Pamela Gayle explores the history of Jamaica from its early days, through the time of foreign powers' conquest, and up to the present day. Covering interesting topics including agriculture, tourism and its impact on the land and people, traditional foods, and the history of some of the names of cities and regions in Jamaica, the book provides a comprehensive look at many elements of the country. Intertwined with that part of its history, the author also reveals the history of some African tribes and how their history relates to the systematic enslavement of people who were then brought to Jamaica as a pass-through before being dispersed into America. Jamaica's location made it a target for slave traders bringing people across the Atlantic, separating them, and then selling them - all under the most unthinkable, brutal, and dehumanizing circumstances. Today, Jamaica is still recovering and recreating its own identity apart from the British Empire and other influences that do not reflect the spirit or culture of its people.

Author Pamela Gayle organizes her content well in The Black History Truth: Jamaica. She moves through the history and cultural highlights and geographically important information that gives the reader a clear look at Jamaica. The combination of text and visual graphics is done well and helps the reader to see the things she is describing. She handles difficult topics with truth and clarity, revealing the endless atrocities endured by many different peoples, tribes, and families as well as those responsible for the atrocities. I appreciate the way the author highlights and showcases the many beautiful and magical parts of Jamaica and Jamaican culture.

Reviewed by K.C. Finn for Readers' Favourite:
The Black History Truth - Jamaica: The Sharpest Thorn in Britain's Caribbean Colonies is a work of non-fiction focusing on historical, cultural, and social issues. It is intended for the general adult reading audience and was penned by author Pamela Gayle to be more representative of the accurate history of the real people of Jamaica, rather than the whitewashed Eurocentric history we have been forced toward in the 20th-century world of education. Exploring the time between the 16th and 19th centuries when Jamaica was a part of the British colonial empire, the work seeks to uncover racial injustices and celebrate the roots of the many different black cultures rising from Jamaica over the years.

Author Pamela Gayle has crafted a sensitive and deeply passionate work of historical non-fiction that seeks to right many wrongs in the world of history education, to highlight black struggles whilst also celebrating black culture and its triumph over intense adversity. Works like these make me deeply ashamed to be British, as well they should, and should continue to do so until we have accurate representation everywhere. The organization of the work, powerful and confident narrative voice, and inclusion of details on important questions such as crime and punishment, culture, belief systems, and historical contention are all marvellously handled and could be used as an example to future historians to model a better future. Overall, I would highly recommend The Black History Truth – Jamaica for any history enthusiast who is interested in exploring the world more authentically and seeing many different sides of the colonization.

Dedications

In loving memory of my father, I know he would be proud of me and his grandson. I wish he was around here today to see how everything has turned out. This book is also dedicated to my son, a wonderful, hardworking and creative young man; my siblings, my aunty and many cousins as well as my very good friends.

Introduction: The Black History Truth: JAMAICA
The Sharpest Thorn in Britain's Caribbean Colonies

This is the second introductory book about the historic events that happened in Jamaica. It has been written to:

- provide a visual glimpse and introduction into the Black presence up to the end of the 19th century
- identify distortions of African peoples, the sanitised myths of the British commercial exploitation and colonialism
- recognise some cultural legacies of colonialism and those that lasted beyond Britain's colonial rule
- stimulate and motivate interest because Black History is for everyone and is part of world history

As this provides a short introduction, it is hoped that young people will find the contents stimulating enough to further their Black History education, and become empowered as a result of their knowledge and understanding. It is hoped that adults will read this introductory book and share their knowledge. It is further hoped that educators find this book useful as a resource. Each theme is one page long, starts with a question, and uses visuals to inspire. Themes are reviewed and critiqued using primary and expert secondary sources.

This book explores how enslavement began in Jamaica as the demand of tropical goods increased exponentially. It is an overview of the historical root cause of British invasion, which was based on plunder, trade and violence. That violence was so deeply entrenched that it became normalised for whites and the descendants of former captives.

Most historical sources and illustrations were written and drawn by white men (a few were white women as well) who were royals, conquistadors, officials, missionaries, travellers, explorers and church ministers. Overseers, planters, merchants, traders and professionals are all referred to in this book, as 'slavers'.

It is important not to bring modern attitudes to the past but readers should be aware that historical sources contain the "cultural and racial arrogances" of white peoples' eurocentric viewpoints. Thus, eurocentric perspectives should be kept in mind, knowing that it ignores and distorts accounts of African and Indian peoples' history. Whilst revealing factual information, their attitudes and perceptions of that period.

Unlike the first book, *The Black History Truth: Argentina*, learning activities are not included within this book, except for a few regarding the contents of original chattel enslavement documents on pages 34 and 35.

**Remember, there is always a reason why things are the way they are.
Focus on and celebrate the strength of the human spirit**

Contents 1

Contents 2

Chapter 1

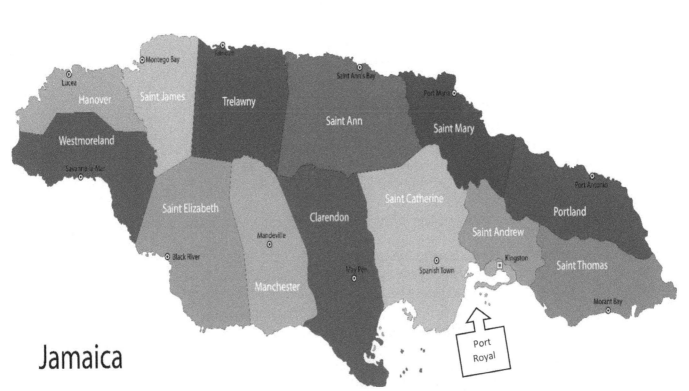

Jamaica

Image 2: © Map of Jamaica with the parishes and their capital cities

Where in the world is Jamaica?

Jamaica is the largest English-speaking tropical island in the Western Hemisphere. The official language is English, spoken as Jamaican English, but experts also believe that Jamaican Patios should be an official language (JIS 2019).

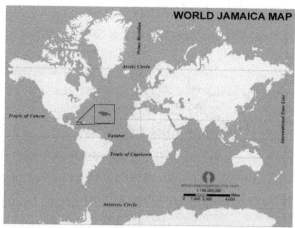

Image 3: World Map showing the location of Jamaica

By 1750, Jamaica was the "Jewel" in the British Crown that was: 'Founded in blood', declared eminent historian, Professor Richard S Dunn (1972), 'from a violent pirate haven into the sugar power of the British Empire'. He also said that: 'Between 1676-1700, ... 77,100 enslaved labourers were brought to Jamaica'. By 1825, there were over one million enslaved people but only 323,000 approximately remained by emancipation.

Continent: Located between the North and South America continents and 90 miles south of Cuba. Experts believe Jamaica is in the North American continent. The island is volcanic in origin. 65-50 million years ago, 'mountains rose up from the seafloor and some land areas sunk'. 12-2 million years ago, 'the island ... emerged from the sea and resulted in the formation of the karst landscape in the Cockpit Country and the deposition of bauxite', according to Wendy Lee (JEPA 2006). Jamaica was once the leading producer of bauxite, described as the "miracle metal", used from pots and pans to trains, planes and automobiles.

The Caribbean: Thousands of islands that were once known as The West Indies, are now called The Caribbean. These islands are divided into three major archipelagos; Greater Antilles, Lesser Antilles and The Bahama Archipelago. The Turks and Caicos Islands became a dependency of Jamaica in 1874', (National Archives CO 137), benefitting from their salt trade until 1959. The Cayman Islands were also administered by Jamaica until 1959.

The Caribbean Sea: The world's second largest, warmest and deepest blue sea with about twenty-five habitable islands. The Caribbean Sea is part of and flows into the Atlantic Ocean where the British slave trade took place. The trade winds and ocean currents shaped how people sailed, inhabited and voyaged around the Caribbean. Jamaicans call trade winds Doctor Breezes during the day or Undertaker Breezes at night time.

The Greater Antilles: The largest and oldest island group that includes Jamaica, Cuba, Haiti and Dominican Republic (Hispaniola), Puerto Rico and the Cayman Islands. The Lesser Antilles contain smaller islands which are further divided into Windward Islands, nearest to South America (towards the winds), and the Leeward Islands (away from the winds).

Island of Jamaica: Shaped similar to a turtle and surrounded by reef-lined beaches and warm seas. 'Jamaica's territory extends beyond its coastline to comprise some 66 islands, rocks and cays', (JIS Parish Profiles). The main geographic regions are 'the eastern mountains, the central valleys and plateaus, and the coastal plains', according to WorldAtlas (2021) and that the 'mountains [were] formed by a metamorphic central ridge of rock from east to west'. The wide expanse of mountainous regions meant that enslaved people could hide and survive away from invaders, successfully.

Tropical Temperatures: Range between 19-32 degrees Celsius, but in 2019, temperatures rose to nearly 40 degrees Celsius in Kingston. Mountainous regions are cooler than coastal plains. Seasons are wet or dry. Short, afternoon thunderstorms are frequent in the wet season. Jamaica is in the hurricane zone from July to September. '1559 was the earliest reference to a hurricane', (NLJ History Notes n.d.). At category 5, Hurricane Gilbert in 1988, wreaked havoc on Jamaica, wiping out 'the entire 7,500 acres of the crop of export bananas', and 'causing US$4 billion worth of damage' (NLJ n.d.).

How big is Jamaica?

Jamaica was Britain's wealthiest Caribbean island, known locally as JA. It is the third largest island in the Caribbean Sea; 235 km long by 82 km wide with an area about 11,000 km^2, whilst the United Kingdom is about 242,900 km^2. So, Jamaica can fit about 22 times inside the United Kingdom!

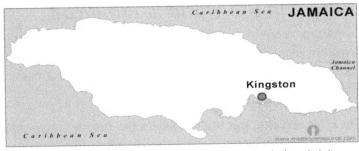

Image 4: Map of Jamaica showing the location of Kingston, today's capital city.

JA has three international airports; Norman Manley (Kingston), Sangster (Montego Bay) and Ian Fleming Airport (Ocho Rios). In 2020, the UK's population was almost 68 million whilst JA's population was not even 3 million. Generally, women live longer; about 83 years (UK) and 76 (JA). Men live to about 80 years (UK) and about 73 in JA, (Worldometers.info 2021); although the world's oldest person and oldest woman died in Jamaica in 2017 at aged 117! Jamaica is now ranked on the 'high human development' category, (United Nations 2019) and 'is classified as an upper middle-income economy', (WHO 2018) with rural inequalities to overcome.

Jamaica was split into three English counties in 1758 during the governorship of a Jamaican Englishman named, Sir Henry Moore. Today, Queen Elizabeth II is Head of State and described as Her Majesty the Queen in Right of Jamaica, since 6 August 1962. Some believe that the Queen should be removed. Professor Carolyn Cooper (UWI) said that 'hanging on to … vestiges of empire in 21st century is ridiculous', reported in the *Express.co.uk* (Charlie Pittock 2021). The Jamaican counties are:

1. Cornwall county: located in the far south western corners, in both England and Jamaica. 'Many Scottish "sojourners" settled … in Jamaica', wrote historian, Dr Nadine Hunt (2010), 'particularly in Cornwall'. The Voyages Database reveal that about 55,464 enslaved Africans, disembarked in Cornwall between 1751 and 1808. Dr Hunt also calculated that: 'In total, 166,914 enslaved people laboured on … estates and plantations', which comprised '59 percent in Western Jamaica'.

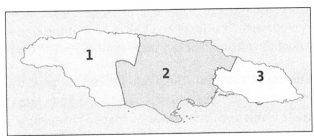

Image 5: Jamaican map showing counties

2. Middlesex county: located 'between the East and West Saxons', according to Encyclopedia Britannica (2020). Hence, Middlesex in Jamaica is in the middle of the Cornwall and Surrey counties, similar to the position in England. The capital of Middlesex County is May Pen in Clarendon Parish; named after Reverend William May, who bred livestock. Pens were 'farms' on land that may have been unsuitable for growing sugar cane, so livestock were bred instead.

3. Surrey county: located in the eastern region. Surrey was known as *"Sutherige"* or southern kingdom by the Saxons. Jamaica's capital city Kingston, is 'a blending of the words "king's" and "town", [because] the English king at that time was William III (1689-1702)', (World Fact Book 2021). The coronation of the English kings, took place in an English town, called Kingston-Upon-Thames, in the English county of Surrey in England. Kingston became the center of trade for the entire British colony due to its natural harbour, the 7th largest in the world from around the 1750s, but is now severely polluted.

Today, 1.2m people (2019 estimate) live within the greater *"King's Town"* area. It is a UNESCO Creative City of Music; where contemporary art, theatre and dance thrive; where Jamaica's first Black millionaire, George Stiebel's home (1820-1896) is located, called Devon House and where Museums, National Stadium, Arena, Emancipation and National Heroes Parks and Cultural Heritage Yards are located.

What have the Brits, Scots, Irish, Welsh got to do with Jamaica?

They left their names in the fourteen parishes to 'control the enslaved, for slavers' security, and easy access to ports solely for the European slave trade', said Dr Andrew Wheatley (*Jamaican Observer 2021*).

Dr Wheatley, an MP, said it was 'a distinct honour to designate [Portmore, near Kingston] the first parish in Jamaica not named after an English king, his wife or some other English personality'! NLJ and JIS Place Names stated that:

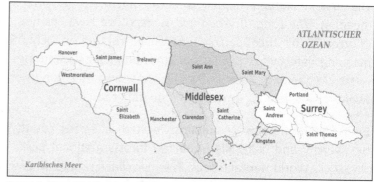
Image 6: Map of 14 Parishes of Jamaica in their counties

Saint Ann's parish: named after Ann Hyde, wife of the British James II. Or a corruption of Santa Ana from the Spanish invasion in 1509. Where the first Spanish settlement of Seville La Nueva, the first sugar mills and earliest Taíno Indian settlements were located. Cardiff Hall, erected by enslaved labour, is named after the capital city of Wales. Edinburgh Castle, now in ruins, was built about 1760 by a "mad Scottish doctor", called Lewis Hutchinson, (JNHT 2011).

Saint Catherine's parish: named after Princess Katherine of Portugal who married King Charles II. The first capital was Jago De La Vega in 1534. The British renamed the capital Spanish Town in 1655. Colbeck Castle, now in ruins, was built about 1680 by English settler, John Colbeck, as protection against Maroon attacks (JNHT 2011). Swansea Town, 41km from Kingston, was named after a Welsh city in Britain.

Saint Andrew's parish: named after the patron saint of Scotland but initially named 'Liguanea', from the Taíno Indian word for iguana. Stirling Castle was named after John Stirling from Scotland, UK. Dublin Castle, now in ruins, is named after the capital city in Ireland. *Half-Way-Tree,* originally named after a 300-year-old massive cotton tree, at the junction of four roads and halfway between where English soldiers camped and the Spanish Town fort. King Edward's memorial clock, on an imposing tower, has now replaced the old cotton tree.

Saint Thomas's parish: named after either Sir Thomas Modyford or Thomas Hickman-Lord Windsor, two governors of Jamaica. Said to be the oldest parish and densely populated by the Taínos. Belfast Town is named after Northern Ireland's capital city of Belfast.

Saint James's parish: named after James, the British Duke of York. Tulloch Town was named after John Tulloch from Scotland. One of the richest parishes when sugar cane made Jamaica the wealthiest English colony. Spanish *"Bahía de Mantega"* (Montego Bay) the capital, meant hog's butter or pork fat, named from the abundance of wild hogs in the area.

Saint Elizabeth's parish: named after Sir Thomas Modyford's wife, Elizabeth. Aberdeen Town was named after Alexander Forbes' home town of Aberdeen in Scotland. Donegal and Kildare place names came from the Irish counties. *I-No-Call-You-No-Come* is a Maroon place name, meant to deter enemies. Balaclava Town is named after the Crimean War and the Jamaican nurse, Mary Seacole.

Manchester parish: named after the British William Montagu, Duke of Manchester who was the governor of Jamaica from 1808 to 1827. The capital is Mandeville, named after his son Lord Mandeville (George Montagu) in 1816. Ballyholly is an Irish place name. Victoria Town, was named after Queen Victoria. *Put-Together-Corner*, near Mandeville, is the place where higgler women stopped to put their goods, and their dress, in order before proceeding to town.

However, the truth be told that nearly all of Jamaica's place names are reminders of its turbulent but rich history.

Why is Jamaica the land of wood and water?

The first inhabitants named Jamaica, *"Xaymaica" or "Yamaye"*, meaning *"The Land of Wood and Waters"*, or it was named *"Las Chorreras"* by the Spanish (English corruption is Ocho Rios) meaning waterfalls or just falls, or land abounding with springs and rivers. Abounding, because Jamaica has over one hundred and twenty rivers, rushing down from mountain sources.

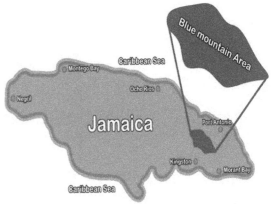

Blue and John Crow Mountains, located in Surrey county, are biodiversity and culturally protected forests, national parks and UNESCO's World Heritage Sites. They 'provided refuge first for the indigenous Taínos fleeing slavery and then for Maroons', and that they contain, 'a high proportion of endemic plant species, especially lichens, mosses and certain flowering plants'.

Blue Mountain peak is 2256 metres; higher than Ben Nevis Mountain in Scotland, UK which is 1345 metres. Today, this climate produces the unique and most expensive Jamaican beverage, known as Blue Mountain Coffee.

Waterfalls that 'flow at high speed', according to the NLJ Handbook, such as: Dunn's River Waterfalls in Middlesex county, that rises to over 183 metres and falls directly into the Caribbean Sea. A popular tourist activity is to climb up and down and under these falls. Water sports take place on the Rio Minho in Clarendon parish, the longest river at 92.5m.

Image 7: Location Map and view of the Blue Mountains.

Milk River Baths, also in Clarendon parish is warm, saline and radioactive. Said to be discovered by an enslaved person whose wounds healed rapidly after a flogging. Martha Brae River, in Trelawny Parish, is popular for its nine metre bamboo rafts, through the tropical rain forest and where James Bond leapt across crocodiles in the *Live and Let Die* film.

Rainforests and Caves: Fern Gully rainforest, in St Ann's, is a magical 5km stretch of road with huge canopies of towering trees, massive leaves and plants crisscrossing the road to Kingston. Green Grotto Cave, is one cave out of 1200, and featured in James Bond's *Live and Let Die* film. It has unique rock formations; 1,525 metres long and 12 metres deep (Cave Register 2020). Dryland Cave in St Mary's parish, was the earliest known Taíno petroglyph (rock carving) site according to the experts. The Taínos buried their dead in caves giving rise to today's Jamaican "Duppy", (soul or ghost) tradition. Later, caves were places where fugitive seekers took refuge to hide from the invaders, slavers and colonists.

Cockpit Country: Located in Cornwall county, and contains 'harsh, dramatic landscape filled with endless hills', according to the World Atlas (2020). It is Jamaica's largest rainforest, made from white limestone (chalk) rocks, with deep sinkholes and shallow caves carved out by rainwater called "karst".

The truth is, that the wood and water landscape of Jamaica provided opportunities for enslaved people to retain their freedom. Freedom seekers lived among the multitude of sinkholes, rainforests, mountains and caves in Jamaica. **Juan de Bolas Mountain** (833m) in Clarendon parish is named after one of the first leaders of the Maroon communities. It was the Maroons, who proved to be one of the sharpest thorns in the British colonisation plans.

Why are pineapples, a cunny bud and soap, national symbols?

Out of Many, One People is the National Motto on the Coat of Arms. The motto was changed in 1962 from its demeaning Latin *"Indus Uterque Serviet Uni"*; meaning servitude of the Taínos to the colonisers. But the truth is, 90% or more are of African descent, so out of which people does "out of many" refer to?

The **Coat of Arms** was designed by Archbishop of Canterbury, William Sancroft in 1661-2. The red cross represents the British Saint Patrick. Pineapples were not indigenous to Jamaica but from South America. Shown on the shield as symbols of "exotic" hospitality at first contact. So much so, that Christopher Wren put pineapple finials on the towers of St Paul's Cathedral in 1666!

Male and Female Taínos, are the original peoples of Jamaica, standing either side of the shield as first peoples. However, they are not extinct. This is an eurocentric myth begun by whites and believed by some Black people.

Crocodile *Crocodylus acutus* on the log, is the largest original reptile. Some believe it symbolises Jamaican people as "dangerous animals" and should be removed. These crocodiles are not the dangerous type, though and are protected by CITES. About 300 live among the mangrove swamps in Black River of St Elizabeth, were many enslaved people landed. Now crocodile tourist safaris take place on large bamboo rafts amongst the lush vegetation and wildlife.

Image 8: National Symbols. Above: Coat of Arms from UWI chapel ceiling. Middle: Doctor Bird. Below: Lignum Vitae flower

Swallow-Tail Hummingbird, Trochilus Polytmus is the National Bird and endemic to Jamaica. Shimmering green in colour with black long tail feathers and long red bills. They create high humming sounds when hovering and fly backwards. JIS (2013) described the hummingbird as Doctor Bird, because the 'erect black crest and tails resemble the top hat and long tail coats doctors used to wear in the old days'. Or, 'the belief ... that the bird was the reincarnation of dead souls ... manifested in a folk song'. The lyrics of which said: 'Doctor Bud, a cunny bud, hard bud fe dead', meaning it is a clever bird which cannot be easily killed.

Lignum vitae, *Guaiacum officinale*, is the National Flower. The flowers are bright blue but fade to white. African-American Dr Steve Buckridge (2003) said that: 'Lignum vitae leaves were used to refresh faded fabric colours'. Dyes and juices from plants allowed enslaved women to "nice up", as he puts it, 'the drab and plain clothing' received from slavers. Moreover, the Maroons used Lignum vitae innovatively, as camouflage, to defeat the British forces successfully.

> *... observed the [Negroes] strange custom of bathing 'in fair water every day, as often as conveniently they can.* Quote 1: Hans Sloane 1707

Lignum vitae also leaves created suds that the enslaved used as soap. Although some enslaved were demoralised by their oppressive conditions; the truth is that, the mass of white British poor, lived in squalor. It was the West Africans who brought Europeans to the frequency of bathing and cleaning clothes with soap. African palm oil, a major ingredient of soap, became 'one of Britain's "new vogues" of washing with soap', according to emeritus Professor of History, David Northrup (1976). E.g., exports of West African palm oil to Liverpool jumped from 3,000 tons in 1819 to 13,600 tons by 1839 and more than 40-42,000 tons by the 1860s (in David Northrup).

The truth is, however, that National Symbols were needed to achieve a unique and distinct national identity as Jamaicans as well as show allegiance to their country after hundreds of years of British enslavement and colonisation.

What is the meaning of the Jamaican flag and one love illusion?

The National Flag means: 'The sun shineth, the land is green and the people are strong and creative', according to NLJ (National Symbols). Before 1962, Jamaica's flag was blue with the Union Jack in the right top corner.

The current flag was created for independence as Jamaica was no longer Britain's colony from 6 August 1962. The colours gold and black were agreed, but the third colour was disputed as most of the 'parliamentary committee … did not want any colour from the Union Jack; so green was chosen', (NLJ n.d.). The gold cross represents Scotland. Reverend William R.F. McGhie, a Church of Scotland minister in 1957 believed that it was important for Jamaica, as a "Christian country", to include the **St Andrew's Cross** from **Scotland's flag**.

Image 9: © Usain Bolt and team celebrate their world record, draped in the Jamaican Flag.

On Emancipation Day (August), Independence Day (August), National Heroes' Day (October), flag raising and lowering ceremonies take place. National Heroes' Day replaced Queen Elizabeth's Birthday in 1965, as the centenary celebration of the 1865 Morant Bay Freedom Movement. Her Majesty's current representative in Jamaica, Patrick Allen said that: 'We must believe in our people, our land and our heritage, and, encouraged by the knowledge of the strength and courage of our heroes'.

- **Green:** triangles at the top and bottom represents hope, agriculture and the lush vegetation on the island.
- **Gold:** St Andrew's Scottish diagonal cross represents the natural resources and beauty of the sunlight.
- **Black:** triangles at the flag and hoist sides represents strength and creativity.

The truth is that, the Jamaican flag is one of only two flags in the world without any of the British Empire colours, of red, white or blue! But it was: **'The phenomenal global success of the nation's athletes … [that] has catapulted the flag to iconic world status'**, (NLJ, National Symbols).

One Love Illusion: In 2019, 4.3 million tourists visited Jamaica earning US$3.64 billion (JTB 2020), but only overseas companies profited. Historically, the North coast made for quick movement of plantation goods to Britain due to its natural harbours and where Cristóbal Colón landed. But although, Jamaica is the birthplace of the all-inclusive paradise holidays, keeping "paradise illusions" alive meant that locals were barred from the finest beaches and waterways; experienced power cuts as well as infrastructure problems and did not meet each other.

Despite employment via tourism, it does not solve the significant underemployment of seasonal work and low pay. Some experts believe that this is a form of neo-colonialism, due to the leakage of tourist dollars, environmental pollution, high unemployment rates and national debt. Furthermore, climate change is unequivocal (IPCC, 2007), meaning beach erosion, warmer days and nights, less rainfall, more hurricanes, increases in sea levels, removal of coral reefs and wetlands, along with increased water usage and solid waste, and water pollution in resort areas will increase, as shown by IPCC (2007).

So, beach erosion may erode "all inclusive paradise illusions" eventually. To counteract this, a ban on most plastics has taken place because: 'Scientists predict that by 2030, there will be more plastic than fish in the ocean', (NEPA 2011). Therefore, changing "paradise illusions" to authentic interior and inland heritage experiences with qualified locals, will only benefit Jamaica, its people as well as challenge negative stereotypes, climate change and neo-colonialism.

What is Jamaica's red gold and blue mahoe?

Bauxite (locally called "backside") is a natural resource in the hills of Jamaica. Mining bauxite ore produces aluminium; once known as the "Red Gold", said Tania Mott, (Commonwealth Law Bulletin 2016).

'By 1970s, Jamaica was the largest [bauxite source] in the world, producing 12 million tonnes of bauxite per year', wrote Guyanese-Jamaican Professor Claremont Kirton (1992), but mining did little to improve the lives of ordinary Jamaicans, only the multi-national US and Canadian companies profited. Today, Jamaica is the sixth leading producer of Bauxite, as indicated by the Jamaica Bauxite Institute (2018).

From Jamaican bauxite, thousands of aluminium products are made overseas. Such as electrical appliances, drink cans, and vehicles (including military vehicles) in other countries. Also called "Red Dirt", due to bauxite waste causing red dust pollution in the air, in water and in soil, resulting in red mud.

Neil MacDonald for Oxfam (1990) recounted challenges between the poor and powerful. The powerful whites wanted the farmers' land situated between the Monymusk Sugar Refinery, in Clarendon, once owned by English sugar giants, Tate and Lyle, and the Clarendon Sugar Company. But the farmers fought for ten years to keep their farming land.

JAMAICA'S BAUXITE TRADE.— Bauxite mining is now the largest single contributor o the export trade of Jamaica and in 1962 was responsible for nearly 50 per cent of the island's domestic exports in terms of money value, says Barclays Bank D.C.O. from Kingston. Bauxite production in 1962 amounted to 7,500,000 tons —nearly a million tons more than in 1961.

Image 10: Above: A winding road of red mud. Below-Jamaica's Bauxite Trade. Times (London, England: 1788), 1963 p.18

'The big men at Monymusk wanted it and we fought them bitterly. When they found we had the land they shut off the [irrigation] water', reported one farmer to Oxfam. Eventually the farmers received compensation as the peasant farmers demonstrated the Jamaican strength of character; fought the sugar giants and refused to give up their land.

Blue Mahoe (Hibiscus elatus)- National Tree

Mahoe is a Kalinago (Carib) Indian word with special qualities that made it the National Tree. 'The 'blue' refers to blue-green streaks in the polished wood, giving it a distinctive appearance', according to JIS (National Symbols), and that 'these trees grow quickly, to more than 20 metres in height and have large heart-shaped leaves'.

The Mahoe tree has many layers that can be separated into bark and fibres to make, 'whips for driving animals and to beat or punish slaves', according to 18th-century Edward Long (1774), a British slaver, colonial administrator, historian and author. He also observed that: 'Jamaicans dyed fabrics with juices extracted from various roots and plants just as their African ancestors did'. Long further commented that the enslaved people are 'extremely dexterous in making caps, ruffles and complete suits of lace with it'.

The bark of the tree is very tough, and not much inferior to either hemp, or flax, on many occasions: it is naturally white, and of a fine, soft, filamentous texture; .... The negroes, and country people, make all their ropes of it; which, had they been tarred and well twisted ...

Quote 2: Patrick Browne (1756) The Civil and Natural History of Jamaica, London

Blue Mahoe is indigenous to Jamaica; used in cabinet-making, construction and decorative objects because it is hard and durable. Wealthy slavers, who built grand country houses in Britain with their fortunes, filled them with quality furniture made from the wood of the Blue Mahoe tree. Moreover, Blue Mahoe is used extensively in reforestation that have been depleted by bauxite mining as it grows swiftly but numbers have been reduced due to heavy cutting in the past.

Chapter 2

Image 11: ©Johannes Lerii's Account of the Caraibe Indians, from 'Americae', 1593, written and engraved by Theodor de Bry (1525-75).

'Theodore de Bry's copper engravings of the living conditions and dress of New World natives were best sellers', explained Professor Patricia Seed

Who were the Jamaicans at first contact?

The Taíno Indians. Archaeological evidence showed that Jamaica was populated much later than other islands and is the youngest Greater Antilles island. Millions of years ago, experts believe that Jamaica was once connected by a land bridge to North America.

Dr William Keegan (2019), an expert anthropologist, wrote that Jamaica may have been 'submerged due to sea-level rise or tectonic activity', and that 'Jamaica was less visible to other islands due to wind and sea current patterns'.

Jamaican Redware Culture, as shown by geologist, Dr James Lee, (1976) produced bright red boat-shaped earthenware potteries, found in St Ann's and Manchester parishes and radiocarbon dated about 1300 years ago. Genetic evidence has also identified that the Redware culture crossed the Caribbean Sea into Hispaniola, Puerto Rico and then lastly, into Jamaica about 1,400 years ago.

Ni-taíno or Ta-íno or Carib or Island Arawak, or Arawak (also spelt Aruaco) or Indian or Aborigine or Amerindian were names given by the invaders. However, Taínos were falsely referred to as the Arawaks of South America. This myth is still prevalent, today.

The truth is that Arawak is a language; 'the largest linguistic group in South America', according to Professor, Dr David Burley (2017). '[T]he Taínos are not one ethnic group, but ... many different

Image 12: Above: ©Taíno Bowl 13th–15th century, depicting zoomorphic characters. Below: the original peoples of Jamaica who evolved into the Maroons in later centuries

Indigenous, Arawakan-speaking peoples who had blended their cultural traits, values and beliefs, and their genes together ... for more than 6,000 years', claimed Jorge Estevez (2016), a Taíno descendant and historian.

Cristóbal Colón's first voyage snatched six or seven people, as proof of a new route to India for Queen Isabella and as translators. Returning a year later, Jorge Estevez's evidence into the origin of the word "Ta-íno", showed that it meant "relative", or "my relatives" or "my friends", or "friends", when Indians on shore and Indians on the returning vessel greeted each other. The Spaniards mistook this as the name of the peoples that they saw.

'Naming a culture by a greeting is not logical at all and is tantamount to saying, "Hello Culture", "Good Day Culture", "Bienvenidos Culture", argued Trinidadian Professor Dr Basil Reid (2009). The invaders 'clearly associated the word "nitaíno" with the Spanish word, "hidalgo", meaning "noble person" in English, a type of knight', said Jorge Estevez. 'That conclusion ... came from Spaniards projecting their own society and its class divisions onto what they thought they saw was the same system among the ... Caribbean peoples'.

Therefore, linking "nitaíno" with the Spanish "hidalgo", the invaders decided that the Taíno people were "noble", but still "savages"; whereas the Caribs were "barbaric" and "cannibals". University Professor of Hispanic Studies, Dr Hilaire Kallendorf wrote that: 'The myth of the Noble Savage is a European myth', only used to justify invaders' exploitation practises. Professor L. Antonio Curet (2014), concluded that the Spaniards operated under, 'an imagined phenomenon'.

What was the myth of the Barbaric Caribs?

According to the Encyclopedia Britannica (2019), the word "Caribbean", was derived from the word "Carib". Carib was the name given to the original Kalinago peoples, of the Leeward Islands. Experts also say the word "Carib" was the origin of the English word, "cannibal".

The Minority Rights Group International (2008) said that: 'The Kalinago people kept Europeans away for nearly two centuries ....' Thus, the Kalinagos (Caribs) were "barbaric", because they had successfully resisted European enslavement with their "strike and sail" resistance strategy, as eminent Barbadian Professor, Sir Hilary McD. Beckles (2008) has shown. But they were demonised because:

Image 13: ©Carib Girls of the Arawak-speaking Parukutu nation. Anthropologist noted: 'It was the daily habit ...to take a bath in the river upon arising in the morning; cover their bodies with paint; oil, comb and decorate their hair; paint designs upon their faces ...and put on their ornaments. The performance would consume an hour at least. In the evening before retiring, they would take a bath and wash off all the paint.'

- Tales of their "barbaric" behaviour sold well in the 16th century and therefore, the invaders lied and or exaggerated their "stories" for sale and profit. University Professor of Literature, Dr Peter Hulme wrote that: 'The old story of ferocious Caribs chasing timid Arawaks ... eating the men and possessing the women, is endlessly repeated in history ... fewer and fewer scholars will accept it'.

- Washington Irving (1828) said that, 'when bones in native dwellings on Hispaniola ... as relics of the deceased, [were] preserved through reverence, but when found amongst the presumed Caribs, they were looked upon with horror as proof of cannibalism', (in John H. McElroy (1981). Ironically, it is argued whether Catholics are symbolic cannibals due to eating Jesus' flesh as bread, and drinking his blood, as wine.

The word Carib ... in Spanish America applied to any wild and savage tribe
Quote 3: Dr John Gifford 1894.

- The Indians bathed regularly to cleanse the soul as well as the body but many Europeans did not. Europeans lived with many domestic animals such as pigs, chickens, as well as rats. They rarely bathed, lived with open sewers and raw human waste for thousands of years. Thus, Europeans suffered from many plagues but also gained some immunity which the original inhabitants of Jamaica did not have. Whites became the carriers of diseases for original peoples.

- Dr Hilaire Kallendorf (1995) confirmed that the: 'Spaniards did not bathe themselves very frequently', and 'remained astonished by the frequency with which the Taínos did so'. Her research demonstrated that the: 'Spanish ... had never supported regular bathing, public or otherwise, associating it with Islam', and that the Spanish believed the, 'custom of bathing oneself so many times could remove a person's energy'.

- Mothers practised head shaping and compressed new born babies foreheads so that it grew backwardly. This was highly admired as beautiful, but offensive to the Spanish, (Dr Kallendorf 1995).

So, Europeans had sufficient myths, distortions and cultural arrogances to exploit and oppress original peoples. The Minority Rights Group International, (2008) confirmed that: 'Missionary accounts prove that such tales of cannibalism were gross exaggerations'. Furthermore, Lisa Hendry of the NHM highlighted that: 'Cannibalism may just have been their way of dealing with dead bodies - different in practice but not in meaning to **cremations, burials and mummifications**'.

Why are Indians always disappearing and declining?

The "vanishing Indian" was an ever-disappearing myth across the Spanish and British Americas where, '"weaker" peoples gave way to "stronger" ones', explained Professor Maximillian C. Forte (2006). However, this myth still continues:

- 'near extinction by 1550', wrote the Encyclopedia Britannica (2020)
- 'rapidly decimated', according to the New World Encyclopedia (2020)
- 'exterminated and replaced by African slaves', said the World FactBook (2021)

> **Doomed to extinction as they "lived a lazy, indolent life".** *Quote 4: James Henry Collens 1896*

The truth is that the "Extinction Story" is a myth of white modernisation. It is the 'Western ideology of progress', according to Dr Forte. But the Taínos who did not vanish must be made 'so insignificant or fraudulent that they also have disappeared'. Additionally, relationships between Spanish men and Taíno women, and their subsequent admixtures with Africans also meant there were "no real Taínos left".

It was Bartolomé de las Casas, (1484-1566), known as "Defender of the Indians", who wrote about the brutality of the Spanish *Encomienda* and *Repartimiento* Indian labour systems. He often used expressions such as, "rapidly exterminated".

Image 14: ©A couple of the Taíno -Arawak people, performing some traditional music to visiting tourists, visiting the Cueva del Indio.

Bartolomé de las Casas' eyewitness accounts were seized upon, translated and transcribed with Spanish biases, compounding inventions on top of fantasies throughout the centuries as shown by Dr Maximilian Forte, until the "vanished Indian" had become official fact. Where ever the invaders colonised, they spread the myth that the Indians were decimated. Dr William Keegan (2019), an expert anthropologist, said that, **'the history books are explicit ... about the total genocide of the Taínos in Jamaica'**.

The truth is that the Spanish colonists blamed the "cannibalistic" Caribs for Taíno extinction and demonised Africans as having polluted and diminished them. This is to justify the importation of Africans, not to replace the exterminated Taínos as eurocentrics believe, but to expand enslavement for more riches whilst simultaneously, commending themselves at converting "savages" to white civilisation. Although, many died from diseases, brutality and overwork, many also fled to the mountains in Jamaica and to other islands.

Taínos are not dead nor extinct!

The ever-declining Indian, is "paper genocide", according to Jorge Estevan, a Taíno and historical researcher, living today in the Dominican Republic. Including Jamaica, Taínos are also found throughout the Greater Antilles, such as Cuba, Haiti and Puerto Rico.

Conversely, Jamaican reporter, Daniel Thwaites critically wrote that, 'after 500 years of intermingling, it's an epic imaginative leap to call oneself Native, [Taíno]', and that people are 'deformed by racism, so, they invent imaginary ancestors of a desired ethnicity'! (*The Gleaner Newspaper*, 2014). Yet the truth is that, in 2018, scientists found a 1000-year-old skeleton with Taíno DNA that, 'counters [the] myth that Taíno population was completely wiped-out', and this is also, 'despite the disruptive effects of European colonisation', revealed scientists Hannes Schroeder and others, (2018).

What is the legacy of the Jamaican Taínos?

Some anthropologists estimated that there were 60,000 Taínos; others up to 100,000; ruled by Caciques (leaders), in over 200 villages. According to Spanish colonists, the Taínos were simple people with a simple way of life.

Taíno Food: They grew 'sweet potatoes, beans, peppers, squash ...', according to Dr Irving Rouse (1992). They fished conch, oysters, crabs using advanced fishing techniques. Cassava, a woody root vegetable, was used for baking cassava (yuca) bread; Jamaicans now call cassava bread "bammy". Today, Jamaica's food is generally spicy. Taíno food preparation known as the "*barbacoa*" (barbecue), using Jamaican pimento, are the origins of the now famous and popular "Jamaican Jerk" tradition.

Taíno religion: The Taíno Indians believed in many gods represented by Zemis. They were superb stone and wood workers and carved Zemis to represent their beliefs (now in the British Museum). 'One of the most spectacular discoveries were three wooden Zemís from Carpenter's Mountain in Manchester parish, found in 1792. They were the *"Bird Man"*, the *"Rain Deity"* and the *"Man with the Canopy"*', according to archaeologist, Dr Joanna Ostapkowicz (2015). She also said that they put the skull and bones of dead bodies in pottery bowls and buried them in caves. The Spanish saw this as evidence of pagan idolatry and cannibalism.

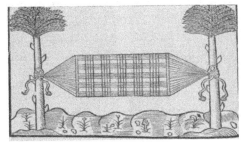

Image 15: Top: Representation of Taíno women preparing cassava bread in 1565: Middle: Dugout canoe used by Taínos as shown by Benzoni 1563. Below: Woodcut of hammock strung between two palm trees. Fernandez de Oviedo y Valdes, Gonzalo, 1478-1557

Taíno Technology: The hammock was adopted by the European slavers to avoid rodents on their rat-infested slaving ships. Conucos are heaps of soil that improved drainage, and delayed erosion so crops were preserved for longer. Taínos were excellent seafarers and built dugout canoes from single logs. There was 'one near Jamaica that held in excess of 100 people', according to Professor of Anthropology, Dr Marshall McKusick (1960) and that 'there was considerable maritime activity', between islands. They weaved cloth and extracted poison from yuca. Plants were used to extract black, white and red dyes, used for ceremonial skin painting and for protection against insect bites.

They have more canoes in Jamaica than in any other part of those regions and the largest ... from a single tree trunk ... decorated ... so that their beauty is wonderful.
Quote 5: Translated from Cristóbal Colón's voyages by Andres Bernaldez, 1930

Taíno houses called Bohios were large circular or square buildings; made with wooden poles, woven straw, palm leaves for roofs to keep cool and wattle and daub for walls. Roofs were thatched and pitch styled, to withstand hurricanes. Other buildings were separate kitchens, ball plazas, temples and canoe sheds called "atarazanas" to avoid sun damage. Caciques' houses were larger with galleries, gabled roofs and decorated.

Taíno Words have entered the English and Spanish languages: *hammock, tobacco, hurricane, barbecue, canoe, sweet potato, barracuda, savanna, maize*, amongst many others. The truth is that, Taínos lived as, 'farmers, potters, and villagers with socially complex societies', according to Trinidadian Professor, Dr Basil Reid (2009). He argued that, the "simple culture" argument only justified in the minds of white eurocentrics, 'the theft of land', and 'guilt associated with the death of a large population'.

Chapter 3

Image 16: The Landing of Columbus in the New World, 1492. ©Painting by William J. Aylward (b.1875).

Who were the Blackamoors?

'Iberia was colonised … in the 8th century … [by] Muslim Arabs and Berbers', wrote Professor Kathleen Deagan (2003). Iberia consisted of Spain and Portugal. Some experts believe that the narrow peninsula of Spain's southern Mediterranean coast, was "almost uninhabited" until the Moorish African army landed in 711. Thus, Iberians were very familiar with African people and African Muslims as *Moors*.

In 1469, King Ferdinand of Portugal married Queen Isabella of Spain. Together, the "Catholic Monarchs", defeated the Moorish capital of Granada by 1492. Then, as Professor Asselin Charles (1995) has shown, 'the Moors are depicted as treacherous, godless pagans, even though theirs was a civilisation that had religion at its center and was technologically superior'.

Image 17: Two Moors 1661. Oil on canvas by Rembrandt van Rijn, 1661.

By 1493, the Pope decreed that the Catholic faith must be spread, in opposition to Islam. Under the pretence of saving souls, the "Voyages of Discovery", had begun. It was no coincidence that the year Iberia gained its independence from the Moors in 1492, that Cristóbal Colón secured royal funding to invade the Americas. Eurocentric historians believe that Moors were *not* an African people, but the truth is that:

> *The Moors of the host wore silks and colourful cloths which they had taken as booty, … their faces were black as pitch, the handsomest among them was black as a cooking-pot*
> Colin Smith. AD 711-1150

1. '"Moor" and "blackamoor"; was any person with dark skin', wrote National Geographic (2019). 'Berber as opposed to "Arab" identity', and 'referring to race, … specifically to African origin', according to Professor Ross Brann (2009); describing 'Muslims who are Africans'. Morisco was "Moor" in Flemish.

2. 'Isidore of Seville, [Archbishop of Seville 636 CE] … follows Roman usage in referring to northwest Africa as Mauritania (from maurus/moro) because, he says, of its inhabitants' blackness', (Professor Brann). Moors are described as '"black", "swarthy," or "tawny" in skin colour … in Othello, Shakespeare's Moor of Venice, (Encyclopedia Britannica (2020).

3. 'The name Moor derives from the ancient tribe of the Maure and their kingdom Mauretania'; 'synonymous with blackness of skin', according to Professor Josiah Blackmore (2006). He continued that: 'Maurus could, from an early date, be a catch-all term for Africans in the pens of western writers'. 'The word moor, with explicit reference to a [B]lack person, occurs 542 times in popular English drama between 1550 and 1642', as shown by Professor of English, Imtiaz Habib (2008).

4. Moor is English; Mohr is German; Maure, Mire, Moros is Italian/Spanish; Mor is Old … English. Furthermore, Black people were known as Saracens in South Italy and Sicily, noted Encyclopedia Britannica (2020).

5. Ancient Iberian DNA research by scientists found that: 'Skeletons from the Muslim era show growing ancestry from both North Africa and **sub-Saharan Africa**', reported in the *New York Times* by Carl Zimmer (2019). Notably though, eurocentric experts past and present, follow the Tropic of Cancer, when labelling Africa as sub-Saharan, really meaning "Black Africa". The origin of which was to divide "Black" from so-called "white" Africa; a stereotypical racist labelling. But the truth is that China also follows the Tropic of Cancer, yet it is not called "Yellow China" or sub-anything by anyone.

Nonetheless, the words "Blackamoor" or "Black moor" or "Black" or "moor" as well as "Ethiopian" were general terms given by whites to name African peoples including the word "Negro".

Who came to serve God and get rich?

Catholics, under the racist "Doctrine of Christian Discovery". In 1455, Pope Nicholas V's papal bull, gave permission for Catholics to seize non-Catholic lands and enslave original peoples.

The Spanish Crown had expelled the Moors in 1492, called the *"Reconquista"*. Then the Catholic Monarchs imposed *"limpieza de sangre"*, meaning purity of blood, from those of Jewish or Moorish ancestry, in their *Reconquista* upon the Americas. Later *"limpieza de sangre"*, was not only religious purity but included imaginary differences between whiteness and blackness.

Image 18: Spaniards enslaving Indians

The Spanish Monarchs, funded Cristóbal Colón's voyages. Eurocentrics believe that Cristóbal Colón "discovered" Jamaica and is commemorated as such. The truth is, people were already living there, centuries before white conquest. Religion was the excuse but they were seeking riches by any means necessary, due to expense of defeating the Moors. Upon this "discovery", many original peoples were killed; overworked; racialised and suffered from diseases, but countless others escaped to the mountains. Their descendants became the sharpest thorns against the British colonialism plans.

The second voyage landed in Jamaica's Discovery Bay (named after Colón's "discovery") on the north coast, in 1494; along with 'sixteen slaving ships; over one thousand men including Cristóbal Colón's brothers, craftsman, farmers, soldiers and livestock', (Encyclopedia.com 2021). That region was densely populated with Taínos settlements.

> *The Indians are so scandalized that nothing can be more hateful or abhorrent to them than the name of Christians.*
> Quote 6: Juan Fernández de Angulo, 1511

> *A miserable Christian, the Crown reasoned, was much better off than a free heathen.* Timothy Yeager (1955)

By 1500, Colón returned to Spain in chains; arrested and thrown in jail with his colonists for embezzlement and torture on Hispaniola. If the locals did not mine enough gold, the colonists chopped their hands off; dismembered bodies and paraded them throughout the villages! Colón was later freed, but carried on with his state sponsored terrorism.

Yet, Cristóbal Colón became a hero in eurocentric modern societies. Other colonists followed; settled in the name of God and glory, but in reality, to extract gold and riches for their own countries. Forced *encomienda* labour and theft of land, built the first Spanish town called **Sevilla La Nueva**, located on approximately 300 acres in St Ann's Bay in St Ann's parish. Then *hidalgos* and itinerants sought their fortunes; by becoming conquistadors in other peoples' lands.

Sevilla La Nueva was renamed **Seville Heritage Park**, and is on the tentative UNESCO World Heritage list because the above events are of "great global significance". **Seville Heritage Park** includes 'the archaeological remains of the Taíno village of Maima, the 16th century Spanish settlement of Sevilla la Nueva, and the post-1655 British sugar plantation', UNESCO (2009). Two events are organised by the JHNT, annually. *Emancipation Jubilee* which commemorates the emancipation of the African enslaved, and *The Encounter* commemorating the park's origins and its first inhabitants.

What is the discovery fallacy?

That Cristóbal Colón "discovered" Jamaica. This is a historical eurocentric fallacy of egotism. But, for eurocentric societies, Cristóbal Colón was the symbol of heroism, bringing great wealth to Europe and "civilisation" to the "backward savages"!

Prices of African gold, salt, pepper, nutmeg and other spices that northern climates could not produce, were taxed by Africans and Arabs in the trans-Sahara Mediterranean caravan trade. That trade flourished for at least five centuries before the British slave trade invasions. This encouraged whites in the medieval period, not only to avoid paying those taxes, but to find quicker routes by sea.

Image 19: Spanish ships, medieval engraving

The truth is that, instead of sailing east towards India, Cristóbal Colón sailed west. He was lost! He then called the people he saw, "Indians". This is why this region used to be called the "West Indies". Whether or not the Taínos could understand their language, was of no consequence because he would kidnap people to become translators. He wrote to Raphael-Sanchez, 14 March 1493 and said: 'I had taken some Indians by force from the first island that I came to, in order that they might learn our language, and communicate to us what they knew .... which plan succeeded excellently'.

1494: Cristóbal Colón's second voyage landed on the North Coast, (now Discovery Bay or Runaway Bay, in St Ann's parish). Born in Italy, he was already a **Portuguese slave trader** ten years before he landed in Jamaica. He said that Jamaica was the, 'fairest islands that eyes have yet to behold ... all full of valleys and fields and plains'.

1498: Panfilo de Narváez was born in Spain; imprisoned for two years for massacring Mexican Indians but became 'one of the island's first settlers', according to Encyclopedia Britannica (2020).

1502-1503: Cristóbal Colón's fourth voyage returned to Jamaica. They were shipwrecked and stranded nearby a "thickly populated" Taíno village of Maima, near St Ann's Bay for one year. Colón died in 1506.

1508: Diego Colón, Cristóbal Colón's son, became Governor of Jamaica. He then appointed Juan de Esquivel; a Spaniard from Spain, to colonise Jamaica.

1509: Jamaica is now a Spanish colony called Santiago. Juan de Esquivel established the first capital, Sevilla la Nueva. It was relocated in 1518, due to the swampy mosquito-filled mangroves and renamed Villa de la Vega. It was renamed again to St Jago de la Vega in 1534 and finally as Spanish Town, by the English after 1655.

1511: Juan de Esquivel did not find any gold in Jamaica. So, the Taínos grew crops for passing ships and other colonies.

1513: First Africans arrived at Sevilla La Nueva and built the first sugar mills. Francisco de Garay was already a slaver before he became the second Governor. Then hundreds of Spanish *hidalgos* rushed to settle in Jamaica. Transients and criminals also hurriedly settled and were, 'said to be the dregs of the earth', as historian, Dr Carla Pestana (2005), has described.

1517: More Africans were imported into Jamaica. They cleared the dense land of forests despite hazardous conditions, constructed forts, roads and slavers' Great Houses. Juan de Esquivel was dismissed afterwards, due to his excessive cruelty.

1555: To break the Spanish-Portuguese monopoly, British Captain John Lok, "carried off four Africans", who were "taule and strong men", (from Ghana) to Britain to learn English as interpreters for the British invaders.

How did the Columbian Exchange affect peoples' lives?

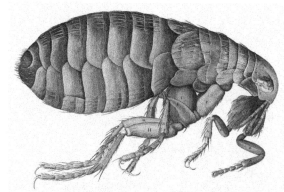

Image 20: Robert Hooke 1655 description of a flea made by magnifying glasses in his book Micrographia.

Diseases, germs, rats, and other stowaways were carried across the Atlantic Ocean in Iberian slaving vessels. Historian Alfred W. Crosby (1972) termed the deliberate and accidental transfer of living species from one continent to another as **The Columbian Exchange**. The Columbian Exchange was the transfer of ideas, plants, animals, diseases and the abduction and forced movement of African peoples between the continents.

In particular, the Caribbean islands became infested with rats that contaminated the food supplies; 'rats of every description, all of them poured from the hulls of Colón's vessels', described historian Charles C. Mann (2012).

Before 1492, 'there were no records of human viral diseases', wrote Professor Francisco Guerra (1993), a Spanish medical historian, but already present in Spain, such as 'influenza, ... smallpox, measles, rubella', but 'not present in the Americas'. Professor Newson (2006), has clarified that 'influenza was carried to Hispaniola by Columbus's second expedition in 1493. This disease originated in pigs, spread to horses and then the passengers, and subsequently to Indians, who died in "infinite numbers".

... diseases were often spread intentionally by Spaniard soldiers to ease the conquests J.M.G. Le Clézio 1988

After 1492, mammals were also deliberately brought to the Caribbean: 'Cows, sheep, goats, horses, donkeys, dogs, swines, multiplied ... in enormous numbers', according to Professor Guerra. It was the '... menagerie of insects, plants, mammals and microorganisms [which] led to infections that the locals had little immunity to', according to Dr Judith A Carney, Professor of Geography. An interesting point was made by Professor Linda A. Newson who said that, **'infections ... have their origin in domesticated animals and then jump the species barrier to become human diseases'.**

The truth is, the lack of access to traditional Taíno food, culture, religion and natural medicines plus the brutal labour of the *encomienda*, meant that the health of many Taíno Indians were severely weakened. Their lifestyles were also significantly changed. However, many others escaped to the mountains of Jamaica as the beginnings of the Maroons.

... all through the land the Indians fell dead everywhere. The stench was very great and pestiferous.

Quote 7: Gonzalo Fernandez de Ovideo y Valdes: 1535.

Today, experts agree that the Columbian Exchange contributed towards climate change and environmental degradation, which negatively affects more people in former colonies than in Europe. Jamaican Professor, Verene Shepherd (2021), said that 'climate crisis had been generated by ... plantation enslavement and centuries of agricultural practices, including mass deforestation'. She also explained that the United Nations Environmental Programme clarified how, **'sugar cane had led to the loss of greater biodiversity than any other single crop in the world, ... because of its impact on ecosystems and increased soil erosion, ... results in the direct loss of species and habitats".**

The truth is that the connection between colonial violence, the Columbian Exchange, climate change and environmental degradation is rooted in the history of white supremacy.

What was the murderous cycle of conquest?

'No encounter in this hemisphere where the Europeans simply traded with the indigenous people on equal terms without invasion, war, conquest, grand theft of land and labour', concluded Professor George E. Tinker, a Native American Taíno scholar. He called this, the **murderous cycle of conquest, murder, thievery and enslavement**.

Bartolomé de las Casas was a 16th century Spanish historian and missionary; the 'first to expose the oppression of original peoples by Europeans in the Americas and to call for the abolition of slavery there', (Encyclopedia Britannica 2021).

Image 21: Life in the Encomienda. Bartolomé de las Casas, "Brief relation of the destruction of the Indies.

Bartolomé de las Casas was originally an *Encomendero,* meaning conquistador. He was rewarded with large areas of Jamaican land and allotments of enslaved Indians, for their participation in the invasions. Taínos had to work for the *Encomenderos* whilst they were converted to "white civilisation", called the *Encomienda* and *Repartimiento*, but due to the brutal atrocities, Bartolomé de las Casas became a Catholic priest instead.

> *They laid bets as to who, with one stroke of the sword, could split a man in two or could cut off his head or spill out his entrails with a single stroke of the pike.*
> Quote 8: Bartolomé de las Casas

Las Casas wrote hundreds of pages of eyewitness accounts about the abuses in the Spanish *Encomienda* and *Repartimiento* labour systems. But eurocentrics believed these accounts were hyperbolic; that is greatly exaggerated. This is because Las Casas revealed his own nation in a "bad light", resulting in other nations labelling the Spanish as the "Black Legend"; meaning Spain was uniquely evil. Hence, officials and eurocentric historians "whitewashed" their own history to suit themselves.

> *... all those that they desired to let live, they would cut off both their hands but leave them hanging by the skin.*
> Quote 9: Destruction of the Indies by Bartolomé de las Casas

Dr Tinker's research and evidence revealed that:
1. Colón kidnapped Indians for Seville slave markets; *meaning that he is a high-level thief*
2. *Encomienda* was a brutal harsh labour regime; *enslavement and theft by another name*
3. European diseases killed many; *meaning Spaniards conquered by invasion of diseases*
4. In Hispaniola, particularly, Indians were 'forced to surrender goods including gold ore; Dr Tinker said that this *'can only be classed as armed robbery'*.
5. Colón's law of tribute required that 'every Taíno over the age of fourteen had to fill a Hawk's bell full of gold every [three] or six months', or 'have their hands cut off; 'which surely meant bleeding to death'; *meaning murder by tribute.*

Accordingly, 'from the beginning', claimed Dr Tinker, 'his mercenary army of marauders engaged in the systematic theft of land, labour, and the natural resources of the indigenous population'. He continued: 'If Cristóbal Colón were alive today, he and his marauding mercenaries would be tried for crimes against humanity'. Today, the proliferation of Torture Museums, filled with macabre instruments of torture, in every European city is testament to the one of the few things that Europeans gave to the "New World" of the Americas. When it comes to torture, genocide and other sorts of human degradation, Europeans gave that to the "New World", say the experts.

What was Asiento de Negroes?

'The monarchy, the government, the church, public opinion in general, supported the slave trade', (Professor Trevor Burnard, Director of The Wilberforce Institute; which spurred on Britain's industrial revolution.

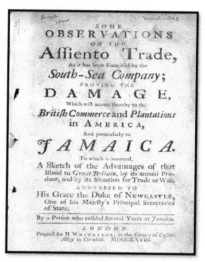

Image 22: South Sea Company document

The Asiento de Negroes was a monopoly contract, at set prices and taxes, between companies and private individuals (Asientists). 'Anyone wishing to sell slaves in the Americas, had to buy licences from the holder of the asiento', according to researcher, Fernando J. C. Mouta (2019).

1494: Spain and Portugal divided the world between them called the **Treaty of Tordesillas.** In the name of God, Gold and Glory, Spain colonised countries to the west, (Americas), while Portugal colonised countries to the east, (Africa, Asia, also Brazil). Spain could not go directly to Africa due to this Treaty. Asiento De Negroes contracts, 1518, provided other national companies or individuals to kidnap Africans for them.

1513: First Africans arrived at Seville La Nueva, (UNESCO 2009) whilst Governor Francisco de Garay, had a five-year asiento agreement.

The Catholick King grants to her Britannick Majesty, exclusive of the subjects of Spain and all others, the Contract of carrying Blacks into the Spanish West-Indies for the Space of Thirty Years, beginning from the first Day of May, 1713, . . . Quote 10: A Collection of Treaties, 1714.

1517: More Africans arrived as servants of the Spanish conquistadors. **1523:** 300 African enslaved; then 700 were ordered, (Dr Patrick Bryan 1992), a Caribbean historian. **1530:** Portuguese-Spanish Jews arrived, fleeing the Spanish Inquisition. **1611:** About 558 Black enslaved, 107 free Black people, and between 1,200-1,400 Spaniards were on the island.

1660: Royal Adventurers Trading to Africa company founded by the Duke of York; trafficked 5,000 enslaved per year; branded with DoY initials. Dutch war led to its collapse.

1672: Royal Africa Company hunted for gold and African peoples, who were branded with RAC initials. An estimated 150,000 captives were abducted from Africa. In 1689, the RAC governor was English slaver, Edward Colston from Bristol, UK, whose prominent statue was "removed" in June 2020. By 1698, the RAC lost its monopoly, opening up to free trade for private merchants, traders and slavers in Glasgow, Liverpool, Bristol, Lancaster and London ports. 1694: 3,000 French men invaded the eastern parishes, but they were defeated.

1711: South Sea Company (SSC) was granted an *asiento* in 1713, under the **Treaty of Utrecht**, to supply 4,800 Africans to Spanish colonies for 30 years. Between 1600 and 1750 about 450,000 Africans were forcibly taken to Spanish America by the British. Englishman, Thomas Guy, founded Guy's Hospital, UK in 1721, with his SSC fortune before its collapse in 1739. Bristol, Liverpool, Glasgow and London were Britain's main slaving ports whilst London also dealt with loans, finances, credits and insurances.

1750: Company of Merchants Trading to Africa, replaced RAC and was active until 1820. By the end of the 18th century, England led the world in the human trafficking of Africans whilst the profits, such as the £260,800 made in 1748 aided the prosperity of Bristol city (Port of Bristol 1749, CO 388 45). Lancaster was the fourth largest slaving port and 'sent more than 180 slave ships out to sea and enslaving more than 29,000 African people between 1736 and 1807 alone', reported the *Lancashire Evening Post*, (Jack Marshall 2021), which made Lancaster a very prosperous industrial 19th century town.

Chapter 4

Image 23: Above-Asante diplomats with swords showing their status.
Below- Igbo Native "Masquerade" Dancers at Awka in the Onitsha Hinterland Between Niger and the Cross River.

Who were the Igbos?

100,000 years ago, people were already living in south eastern Nigeria as shown by Charles Thurstan Shaw, an English archaeologist in 1959. It was, 'an Igbo farmer named Isaiah Anozie [that] chanced upon several bronze objects as he was digging a cistern to hold water in the dry season', claimed the University of Iowa, (1939).

This ancient site, Igbo-Ukwu, revealed 'highly sophisticated work in bronze metalworking', dated from 'at least the 9th century'. The Igbo-Ukwu archaeological site is situated in the modern-day southern Nigeria. Archaeologist Dr Emeka Okonkwo concluded that: 'This mastery of the technical properties of copper alloys by the Igbo-Ukwu traditional metallurgists has not been seen anywhere else in the world'.

Image 24: Above-Map showing European slaving forts. Below- Two of the finest 9th century Igbo-Ukwu bronzes.

Eboes are described as crafty, frugal, disputative, and avaricious; also as haughty, fierce, and stubborn; often manifesting a spirit of despondency ... Quote 11: James Mursell Phillippo (1843)

The Bight of Biafra (Igbo peoples), included the modern-day coasts of eastern Nigeria, Cameroon, Equatorial Guinea, and northern Gabon. Dr Gloria Chuku (2018). Professor of Africana studies observed that, 'prior to 1500, the Igbo had developed a strong economic system based on agriculture, manufacturing, and trade', using 'their technological skills and ingenuity'. They were an agrarian people who 'valued large families and engaged in polygamous marriages'. Wealth was in the land and how much it could produce depended upon a complex hierarchy of servants and relatives.

Dr Gloria Chuku noted that, despite the Igbo's complex lifestyles, eurocentrics described the Igbo people as an, 'amorphous and backward mass', (Margery Perham, Colonial administrator, 1937); 'one of the least disciplined and least intelligible, of African peoples', (Sylvia Leith-Ross, English anthropologist, 1939). The truth is that, their observations were based on "ignorance, racial arrogance and cultural insensitivity", as Dr Gloria Chuku has shown.

After 1776, **Bonny** became Britain's busiest slaving ports: 'Of the 376 vessels from Bonny that arrived in the Americas carrying more than 300 enslaved Africans, 204 disembarked in Jamaica', said historian Dr Stephen D Behrendt (2001). The next busiest ports were the **Old Calabar, New Calabar (Kalabari).**

The Slavery Voyages.org shows that between 1751-1800, 184,350 Igbos (also known as Eboe, Ibo, Moko by slavers) were shipped in Whitehaven, Bristol, Liverpool, and London slaving ships to Jamaica's main towns of Kingston and Montego Bay, from the Bight of Biafra, with an average of 12.5% mortality rate. Professor Douglas B Chambers (2002) said, 'most tended to be Igbo-speaking', as was **Olaudah Equiano**, who later became a well-known Black abolitionist and author.

The truth is that, other groups such as Efik, Ibibio, Idoma and Ga-Adangbe may have adopted the "Igbo" label to blend in with the majority. Evidence shows that Jamaica Patois spoken today, includes words from different African ethnicities. For example, Igbo words, "unu", meaning the plural "you" and "red Igbo", meaning a light skinned person. "Ginal" from the Akan (Ashanti Twi) meaning "con man". The Jamaican "juk" word meaning "to poke", comes from the Fula language. But the word "backra" (buckra), comes from the Efik language of "Mbakára", meaning "white man".

Nonetheless, **before 1776, Akan-speakers from the Gold Coast,** were the dominate groups forcibly taken to Jamaica.

What are the roots of the Jamaican enslaved?

Image 25: Ghana is home to one of the world's only surviving traditional architecture belonging to the Asante people which is one of UNESCO's World Heritage Sites (WHS) according to ©Visit Ghana.com; Typically adorned with Adrinka symbols

Mitochondrial DNA (mtDNA) research has revealed that a large majority of **Jamaicans today, originated from the Gold Coast**. Dr Simon Newman's (2013) mtDNA investigation showed that, 'the Gold Coast was ... the single largest region of origin of the enslaved Africans who arrived and remained in Jamaica, and of their descendants on the island today'.

The Gold Coast, known as **Berkino Faso** and **Ghana** today, was rich in gold, petroleum, crude oil and natural gas that the Europeans used to build up their countries. The Bight of Biafra and Bight of Benin regions also had massive numbers imported as shown by the Voyages Database.

The truth is that the database only lists the coastal African ports shipped from, which is not the same as their true regional origin. For instance, the Akan are, 'divided into the Asante, Fante, Akwapim, Akyem, Akwamu, Ahanta ...', (Ghanaweb, no date). Nonetheless, British slavers considered: 'Gold Coast slaves ... the most valuable of any slaves exported from Africa'. 'The [N]egroes most in demand ... are the gold coast, or as they call them, Cormantines', wrote Dr Newman, or "Cormantees". People shipped from Kormantin village, then became known as the **"Coromantee nation"**, identified as, 'warlike, the head of all insurrections', explained Dr James Delle (2009) but made 'good labourers'.

> ... that the Cormante or gold Coast Negros have always Stood and proved bestt in this plantation theirefor you will doe welle to buy of that Nation than any other. Quote 12: Peter Thomson, 1679

Slavers believed that "Cormantees" had more resilience, stamina and endurance for labour, than other African ethnicities, but were also seen as rebellious. Believed to be so dangerous that the French banned "Cormantees" from their "West Indian" colonies. But the Haiti Revolution has shown, that this strategy did not work!

Yet, the truth is that, Coromantee were not a people in Africa, but the name of a fishing village called Kormantin, according to the experts. Professor Jessica Krug (2014) is adamant that, **'there is in fact no Kormanti [Cormantee] identity in Africa. It is imagined ethnicities on the part of slavers and historians'.**

Even though, 30% of all captives arrived from the Bight of Biafra in contrast to 29% from the Gold Coast into Jamaica, according to the Voyages Database, more Igbo (from Biafra) peoples may have been shipped off the island. Jamaica was a major entrepot to other islands.

> ... more Jamaicans today trace their matrilineal origins to the Gold Coast than to any other region of Africa.
> Dr Simon P Newman (2013)

The truth is, however, that mtDNA evidence does suggest, 'a core population of Gold Coast Africans in Jamaica', (Dr Newman) and that, 'between 1655 and 1739, Gold Coast slaves were held responsible for at least six armed insurrections and innumerable instances of insubordination, flights and suicides'.

The truth is that the Gold Coast captives proved to be a considerable and severe thorns in the British colonisation plans, whether they were "Coromantees", or not.

Where was the first Gold Rush?

In 1471, the Portuguese were so, 'impressed by the flecks of gold that sparkled in the streams south of the Asante Kingdom, that they called the area the "Gold Coast", noted anthropologist Professor Robert B. Edgerton (1995).

Located in today's interior of Ghana and southeastern Côte d'Ivoire, the Asante Kingdom, or Ashanti, is one of the famous West African Kingdoms. Not to be confused with the Ancient Ghana Empire that was located further north and reigned much earlier, between 300 to 1100 CE.

The Ashanti are a subgroup of Akan-speakers and the earliest settlers from about 3500 years ago. They migrated from "prolonged drought prone areas" to the "lush and dense, well-watered forested zones" by the 17th century, according to the experts. In the late 1600s, Kumasi became their capital city.

Image 26: Gold-weight, in Akan-style stool (based on the Golden Stool of Asante; ©The Trustees of the British Museum

Africa is not a "dark continent" nor "uncivilised" nor "without history" as told in eurocentric history books and the media. The first Ashanti King and military leader Asantehene (King of Asantes), 1701 to 1717, Osei Tutu developed, 'elaborate governing institutions, including a judiciary and management of a confederacy of small states', according to the SAGE Encyclopedia of War (2017). For example, Denkyira state was defeated and incorporated into the Ashanti Kingdom, with a new constitution and re-organised military.

'By the end of the eighteenth century, the [kingdom] had … a population between two and three million people', according to SAGE Encyclopedia of War (2017). Ashanti's wealth was driven by agriculture, goods, and land. Success was focused on national unity, 'its people were willing to die, for their king, country, gods and honour'. (Prof. Edgerton 1995).

Ashanti's wealth came from trading gold that was 'plentiful and easy to extract out of the environment', said Christina Griffith (2019) from the Penn Museum, US. From the '16th century, gold traded out of Akan lands totalled over 3.6 million troy ounces (around 112,000 kilograms) per century', according to British archaeologist Dr Amanda Logan (2020) and that their currency was gold dust. Today, however, the New World Encyclopedia (2008) said that: 'Much of the magnificent Asante gold regalia can be seen in London in the British Museum'.

The Asantehene of the Ashanti Kingdom, united people under the legend of the **Golden Stool** that was **"brought from the sky"** in 1698. 'To the Asante, the Golden Stool is so sacred and unique', explained Professor Paul Banahene Adjei (2015), that it was never meant to be sat on, not even by the Asantehenes, as it represented their ancestors.

The **Golden Stool** is kept in secret and local chiefs pledged their allegiance to it. Its reverance, is similar to the 'throne in European monarchies', clarified anthropologist, Dr Beverly Stoeltje (1997); regarded as the spiritual seat of the Ashanti soul. Never sat on, it symbolises the essence of the Ashanti people, their culture and their historical lineage.

However, the Ashanti Kingdom was in a continuous state of war with Britain, between 18th and 19th centuries. It was the British greed for gold, captives and goods that eventually weakened the Kingdom of Ashanti.

Why were Elmina and Cape Castles built?

Europeans wanted protection from each other, from pirates, as head quarters, and to hold captives, that they built coastal forts; São Jorge da Mina, (El Mina, meaning mining for gold), in 1482 and Cape Coast Castle in 1555, using deception, warfare, trickery, bribery or collaborators to sign treaties with Gold Coast rulers.

The British built Fort Charles in 1654 and Annamaboe Castle (known as Fort William) in 1753. Millions of captives were held in the dungeons of these "castles" for weeks, before boarding slaving ships to Jamaica through the **"Doors of No Return"**.

Image 27: Cape Coast Castle, slave trading fortress on the African Gold Coast. Headquarters of the Royal Africa Company (RAC).

Far from the eurocentric notions of "uncivilised savages and timeless barbarians", West African empires and kingdoms were at the forefront of globalisation and innovations. They were some of the first farmers, first iron-workers with their own artistic traditions; functioning democratic or monarchical governmental structures; centuries of trans-Sahara trading in gold, spices, salt, and other commodities, that flourished until the arrival of Europeans. For example: 'By 1500, [the] goldfields of Ghana and Cote d'Ivoire are supplying 30,000 ounces of gold a year to Portugal', according to eminent historian, Toby Green (2019). Indeed, Europeans were 'dazzled', at '[t]he wealth of the royal court [Ghana]', which was 'remarkable, for its lavish display of gold', (Encyclopedia of Cultural Sociology 2012).

The Dutch captured El Mina in 1637, sold it to the British in 1872 until Ghana gained independence in 1957. The Fante and Ashanti elites exploited competition between the European nations for their own benefits, but to the eventual detriment of their communities. However, their traditional rivalry was also exploited by the British who sided with the Fante, to capture more people from the interior who were then held in the castle dungeons.

> Eminent Historian, Professor Toby Green: *West African gold producers had provided the gold that financed the expansion of Mediterranean economies. Ever since around 1000 CE, the gold of Christian Europe and the Muslim world had come largely from West Africa …*

Up to 16,000 people, including the castle enslaved, evolved around these castle forts. Descendants of European men and African women were "Mulattoes" (Spanish), "Tapoeyers" (Dutch), "Luso-Africans" (Portuguese), or "Half-Caste" or "Half-Breed" (British). Professor Kwame Daaku (1970), wrote that, 'mulattoes were among the emergent "new class" of wealthy traders in the booming seventeenth-century Gold Coast trading centres'.

El Mina's coastal biracial or multiracial people had mixed fortunes but most were middlemen or middlewomen. The truth is that, 'the mulattoes played a vital role … between Europeans and Africans on the Gold Coast', argued Professor Rebecca Shumway (2014). With the aid of these descendants, together with African collaborators, captives were tricked or forced into castle dungeons. Some of the captives died in shackles, whilst awaiting their forced emigration.

Today, El Mina is a UNESCO World Heritage Site frequented by thousands of "Back-to-Roots" tourists seeking authentic experiences. Cape Coast Castle is the site of the PANAFEST (Pan African Arts Festival). Diasporic Africans are seeking enlightenment, spiritual or physical well-being to attain peace from the legacies of the traumatic past and present. It may be ironic, however that, these castle forts used to make profit off African bodies and now they exist; to make money from "diasporic Africans", undertaking pilgrimage type tourism.

Who were the Ashanti and Fante?

Image 28: Above -Asante domestic architecture made of clay. Below: Fante thatched-roof housing outside the notorious slave fort at Cape Coast in the Voltaic region.

The **Ashanti (Asante) Kingdom**, was located in the northern interior. At its height, wealth and territory were achieved through agriculture, fishing, palm wine, palm oil, kola nuts (coca cola); pottery; gold, ivory and replica Golden Stools, carved in wood that were 'owned by almost every man, woman, and child in Ashanti', explained British envoy Captain Robert Sutherland Rattray (1927), by the late 18th century.

Englishman Thomas Edward Bowdich (1819), from the African Company of Merchants was, '**surprised to discover that most of these major [Ashanti] structures had indoor toilets that were flushed by pouring gallons of boiling water down them**', stated the Encyclopedia of Anthropology (2006).

Bowdich also described one of Kumasi's (capital city) streets, as 'one hundred yards wide, that was swept and trash collected and burned every day'. He observed that, 'many houses were two-story stone palaces, were large, neat'. Furthermore, he also noted that 'the blacksmiths' forges were always at work'.

The **Fante Kingdom**, in the south, occupied the eighty-mile stretch of Atlantic coast of Elmina, Cape Coast and Annamaboe. The town of **Koromantse** or **Kormantin**, just a few miles from Annamaboe Town, is where the so-called "rebellious Coromantees" are believed to have originated from. But that is not the same as being shipped from the coastal ports of Kalabari or Bonny. Other African ethnicities may have come from different regions, ended up in Kormantin Town and then one onto one of the shipping ports.

British archaeologist, Professor Amanda Logan (2020) wrote that: 'Slaves were captured either through slave catching (i.e., kidnapping) missions or as a byproduct of violent conflict'. For example, Ottobah Cugoano was a twelve-year-old boy kidnapped whilst visiting relatives in 1770. Later, he became a well-known Black abolitionist and author. In 1787 he wrote that: "I was born … on the coast of Fantyn". He described how he was kidnapped: "We went into the woods as usual". Then "several great ruffians came upon us suddenly". Ottobah's evidence showed how "ruffians" used deception, threats, or weapons to march naïve children away to the castle factories.

Moreover, evidence showed that, 'a very high number of children [were] taken aboard slavers' [vessels] in the last years of the nineteenth century', according to Professor Trevor Getz, (2003) although he believed, records were sketchy. 'From 1810 on, and decidedly after 1850, children made up to 40% of cargoes and women a further 15%', confirmed Professor Dr Molefi Asante (2005). The truth is that depopulating the Gold Coast from its young able adults has significantly impacted on the future economic and social health of the Gold Coast and then Ghana in the following decades and centuries.

Yet, the truth is, the root causes of violence, were the Europeans greed for gold, trade, control of the coast against other European nations; as well as the use of enslaved people to extract wealth from the "New World" for their own benefits.

How was Akan society organised?

A contract between families. The society is **matrilineal**, and forms the core of a town and thus the state, according to the experts.

SAGE Encyclopedia of Anthropology (2006) wrote that: 'Queen mothers ... and other women in this matrilineal society have always had important roles in Asante politics'. Ghanaian anthropologist, Thomas E. Kyei, (1992) and British Envoy Captain Robert S. Rattray (1927) identified kinship and linages as:

Image 29: Fanti women, Gold Coast, 1890. Expert genealogists. The New York Public Library

Mother's Lineage: Ashanti (Asante) children, automatically belong to the mother's side of the family. They are related to all their mother's brothers (called uncles) and sisters (called mothers) and the child's mother's parents (grandparents called Nana/Nanni) by blood. A child's first cousins (mother's sisters or brother's children) are siblings because their mother's sister is related to the child's mother by blood. Any inheritances belong to the mother and her blood relatives.

Father's lineage: Ashanti children inherit their father's spirit and soul. The father, is responsible for socialising children and their marriages. The father and his brothers have responsibility for their younger brothers and sisters and his sisters' children; his grandchildren by his sons; his household servants and children of those servants. The father (husband) has little influence over his wife, his own children or grandchildren. Nominated elder males are ultimately the family head.

Wife and husband: live separately in their maternal homes (in extensions) or in their own homes, but visit each other every day. Separations of up to two years due to nursing mothers happens and then subsequent wives take over responsibilities. There is no joint pooling of money. 'a clear sign of Akan women's economic independence and of high status', according to anthropologist, Stefano Boni (2002). Men inherit responsibilities for widows of their late brothers or sisters after a year's mourning. Wives have their own farms and agriculture, as well as assisting their husbands in their ventures. Burials within the house, beneath floors, is a traditional Akan burial practice.

Marriage: both wife and husband must be from a different blood kinfolk and outsiders. The wives' uncles or brothers can intervene if they are unhappy. A man may have more than one wife, approved by all kinfolk. A man may not marry his mother's sister, mother's sister's daughter or mother's sister's daughter's daughter and similar on his father's brother's side, but cross cousins that are his mother's brother's daughter, or his father's sister's daughter are expected. Any blood or spiritual violation of who to marry would jeopardise souls in the after life.

Asafo: (warrior clans, soldiers) were groups of men that evolved as, 'a unique Fante response to circumstances generated during the slave trade era', wrote Professor Rebecca Shumway (2014). Asafo protected against kidnapping and defence against non-Akan groups. Organised along patrilineal lines, Asafos were 'a manifestation of the patrilineage in a predominantly matrilineal society', said Professor Trevor R Getz (2003).

Thus, in Ashanti tradition, those who belong to the same group address one each other as "brothers", "mothers", "uncles" etc. Experts believe that all the seeds of the more advanced system of government, already existed within this family democracy. But interactions with exploitative whites and colonialism, led to these units being systematically corrupted.

Who was Nana Yaa Asantewaa?

The Ashanti leader of the 1900 Ashanti-British war. When the British outlawed slavery on the Gold Coast it, 'crippled the profitability of the African Company of Merchants'. The truth is, the British wanted to stop other nations gaining more power and gold than themselves and therefore, colonisation was the answer.

1823-1831 War: Ashanti defeated the British who had the Fantes as allies.
1863-1864 War: Ashanti defeated the British and occupied the coast.
1873-1874 War: Ashanti were defeated which ended in the Treaty of Fomena.
1894-1896 War: Ashanti were defeated by the British. Leaders were exiled.
1900-1901 War of the Golden Stool: The Kumasi British Govenor, Sir Fredrick Hodgson, demanded that which was not theirs, the Golden Stool. To sit on as 'representative of the British Queen as 'paramount chief', (B Wasserman 1961), to possess it and humiliate the Ashanti. The white supremacist ideology believed that the Golden Stool, was a symbol of power instead of the **"soul of the nation"**.

Nana Yaa Asantewaa (1840-1921), Queen Mother of Ejisu (Edweso), from Asona royal conventional stool lineage, was a major landowner and prosperous farmer. For years, she had spoken out against British harassment; failed years of diplomacy; refusals to return the Asantehene Nana Agyeman Prempeh 1 leader, that had been exiled to the Seychelles.

Image 30: Yaa Asantewaa statute in Ghana. Soldiers traditionally cover their clothes with talismans for luck and protection.

Nana Yaa Asantewaa led the **1900 War** to force the British to return the exiled Asantehene. Previously, the men thought, as their leader was exiled, they did not want to fight. When Yaa Asantewaa told them that women would rise to the challenge if they would not, they became motivated to defend their country.

Nana Yaa Asantewaa's army had early tactical successes through the dense forests which laid between the Ashanti capital of Kumasi (spelt Coomassie by the English) and the coast. The British had to bring in external forces to defeat the Ashanti. The truth is that Yaa Asantewaa was 'the overall leader and Commander-in-Chief of the Asante forces', said Ghanaian historian, Albert A. Boahen (2003). Although, eurocentric historians disputed that she ever went on the battlefields.

Part of Yaa Asantewaa's Speech: *No white man could have dared to speak to the Chief of Asante in the way the governor spoke to you chiefs this morning ... I shall call upon my fellow women. We will fight the white men. We will fight till the last of us falls on the battlefield.* Quote 13: Yaa Asantewaa Speech in Venatius Chukwudum Oforka, (2015)

Nana Yaa Asantewaa surrendered when her daughter and grandchildren were held as British hostages. Then she was exiled to the Seychelles. According to the New World Encyclopedia (2008): 'The British troops plundered the villages, killed much of the population, confiscated their lands and left the remaining population dependent upon the British for survival'. By 1902, the Gold Coast was a British crown colony.

Nana Yaa Asantewaa, known as Africa's Joan of Arc by eurocentrics, successfully defended her nation. Although the British declared victory, the Ashantis, also proclaimed victory as the Golden Stool remained successfully hidden from the British. The truth is that, the impact of her vision and beliefs, stirred eventually into the movement for independence from Britain, to become Ghana (meaning Strong Warrior King) by 1957; the first West African country to do so.

Nana Yaa Asantewaa was a great national heroine of anti colonial struggles; her legacy inspires women to be courageous, independent by not relying on others, determined, and to stand up against injustice collectively.

What is the Odwira Festival?

Since the 17th century, Asantehene Osei Tutu developed the **Odwira Festival**, a symbol of national unity; to purify Ashanti stools, the town and themselves from pollution. Experts also believe it is the **Yam Harvest.** Yams are large long cylindrical root vegetables, covered in a rough tree-like bark with either white or yellow inside; worth $20 million to Ghana's economy today.

'In 1784, Liverpool Captain William Sherwood purchased 16,000-17,000 yams at Bonny', (Assembly of Jamaica 1789). This was to ensure more captives survived the Atlantic graveyard which in turn, safeguarded slavers' profits. Simon Taylor, an 18th-19th century Jamaican sugar tycoon, advised other slavers to arrive at the time of the harvest. He said that yams were, 'the favourite food of all the Eboe Negroes'. So, yams, 'contributed to the nourishment of slaves in the face of oppression and dehumanization', said W.F. Mitchell (2009).

Today, the Ashanti and the Fante are the two largest Akan groups, totalling 11.5 million people or 47.5% of the total population in 2010 (Ghana Statistical Service 2012). The population swells to over 100,000 during the festival in Kumasi. Historically, Odwira consisted of:

Image 31: Above: Yam Festival according to British Thomas E. Bowdich 1819 -Umbrellas are topped with gold emblems... Below: Current festival. Ashanti Chiefs wearing clothes woven in Kente patterns and decked in gold jewellery.

- a procession of priests, giving thanks and offering up yams to the ancestors before new crops of yams are "*nyamed*". "*Nyam*" meaning to eat, is a word Jamaicans use today.
- the mourning of past ancestors and those who had recently died.
- honouring the Ashantehene and Queen and presenting them with gifts.
- purification of the Golden Stool, itself a mass of solid gold; standing on its own throne, to avoid evil spirits entering the Ashantehene's body from the ground.
- people are, "laden with collars, brace-lets, hoops, and chains either of gold, copper, or ivory ... and girdles of blue stones like beads', according to Professor James Anquandah (1999). Participants wear the famous vibrant kente cloths.
- Over 100 Adinkra symbols represent proverbs that appears on gold weights, textiles, such as the kente cloths, and architecture (see Image 1 and Image 25). All the symbols have unique looks and communicate different messages.

The chiefs in the general blaze of splendor and ostentation wore Ashantee cloths of extravagant price, from the costly foreign silks which had been unraveled to weave them in all the varieties of colour as well as pattern; they were of an incredible size and weight and thrown over like the Roman Toga.
Quote 14: British envoy Thomas Bowdich 1819

Englishman Thomas Bowdich (1819), attended the Odwira. He described it as an 'overwhelming sound barrage' of music using ivory tusks of elephants as horn trumpets, flutes, firing blunderbusses, heavy drumming, singing and umbrellas that bounced and danced in time with the music; all representing the dispelling of evil spirits that Bowdich was unaware of.

According to Ghanaian Professor, Edward Addo (2011) the festival demonstrates and pledges allegiance to the kingdom, as well as affirms loyalty to the 'golden stool', which is the embodiment of the soul and power of the kingdom.

What is the rescuing Africans from African slavery myth?

The eurocentric meaning of "slave" originated from the word "slav", from the **Slavonic** peoples of Eastern Europe who were the "slavs" of Muslim Spain. Thus, the word "slav" became synonymous with white slaves, as in Anglo-Saxons (410-1066); Vikings (800-1066); Normans (1066-1154) who all invaded the UK, and enslaved each other in varying forms of enslavement.

Image 32: Iron Collar and Chains Used by Slave Traders, early 19th century

However, despite Africans not practising the white "slav" type slavery, eurocentrics justified their racial slaving atrocities as "rescuing Africans from African slavery". English British envoy and anthropologist Captain Robert S. Rattray (1927) made a significant point. He wrote that people must, **'banish from our thoughts the familiar pictures conjured up in our minds by the popular conception of slavery as it existed in Europe and America prior to its abolition'.**

Ashanti wealth was not only in gold, but land, food, goods and "people", (Dr Judith Spicksley 2013). Those "people" were lost in translations, interpretations and racism to the European degraded meaning of "slave". Guyanese Professor, Walter Rodney (1966) confirmed that the word, "slave" as used by Europeans, was **'so loosely [used] as to apply to all the common people'**. Yet the truth is, that a form of serfdom and class system, already existed in Akan-speaking nations. But the British projected their racial biases onto what they thought they saw and distorted it for their own benefits.

Chattel slavery is a European invention. Chattel comes from the word "cattle"

Pawned bodies in contrast to "slaves", in Gold Coast records were used as "secure safety for goods", "secure future payment", and as "proof of intention or good behaviour", (Dr Judith Spicksley). Pawns were also gold, jewellery, ceremonial and ordinary items, she noted. She commented that the term "pawn", had become generalised to include collateral for loans as "pledges", "hostages", or "sureties".

Household slaves were not the opposite of freedom but the **opposite of kinship**. For Africans, to be without family ties was to be alone and unprotected. Historian, Walter Rodney (1966) said that, they owned plots of land; could marry and have inheritances. British Captain Robert S Rattray (1927) explained that: 'An Ashanti slave, in nine cases out of ten, possibly became an adopted member of the family'. They were **servants in servitude, not "chattel".**

Criminal acts outside kinship groups rather than within the same lineages resulted in capital punishment. Taboos resulted in fines or being run out of town for adultery or immorality. Civil acts of slander, gossip or personal abuse resulted in compensation if proven, because, 'to have a bad name rendered life, ... unbearable', wrote Rattray (1927). War captives were included within the Ashanti kingdom which expanded their territories.

The truth is, Ashanti "law had become warped" (Dr Spicksley 2013). Chattel slavery was unlike any form of African serfdom which involved the denial of the enslaved person's humanity, and on grounds of race alone. The British slave trade created chaos, which eventually turned traditional custom into, 'panyarring, meaning holding hostages for ransom under threat of sale into slavery', according to historian Sarah Balakrishnan (2020) (e.g., kidnapping) as well as raiding and military wars.

Walter Rodney (1966) has demonstrated that eventually, **'there was hardly any offence at all which did not result in the selling of individuals into European hands'!**

29

What is the fallacy of Africans selling Africans?

Image 33: Map from 1896 of the British Gold Coast Colony showing Ashanti (Asante) and other nations according to the Europeans.

Eurocentric whites justified the British slave trade because they believed that "Africans sold Africans". Thus, people from the Gold Coast should be grateful for being "saved" from West African "slavery" and deposited in Jamaica; the stereotype of which, later, became the "grateful slave"! The truth is that:

The continent of Africa has the highest genetic diversity than any other continent. Today, there are more than 200,000 speakers of 130 languages spoken in West Africa alone. The Akan language consists of Ashanti (5 million), Fante (2 million) and Abron (1 million), according to the experts. Thus, one ethnic group may not have any affinity to another group outside of their own ethnicity or language group.

Eminent historian, Professor Michael Craton (1978) highlighted this fallacy. He said that, 'new recruits were taken indiscriminately from tribes as different from each other as Lapps from Basques or Greeks'. Hence, Ashantis or Fantes were just as different to "outsiders" or other "ethnicities".

People from different ethnicities or languages were not openly trusting of each other just as white nations were not. White nations engaged in centuries of wars, from which their warring, aggressive, and materialistic attitudes evolved naturally. In fact, the British and French were at war for 116 years (14th -15th centuries), called "The Hundred Years War". Throughout, weapons of warfare, methods of torture and greed for power and wealth grew and continued into the British slave trade.

The role of the African rulers are exaggerated fallacies of eurocentric distortions. Eurocentric historians tried to justify the chattel enslavement trade by blaming Africans and or their rulers for their own fate. But the truth is that, blaming Africans releases whites from their guilt. Furthermore, trading with African rulers consisted of unscrupulous practices. The typical British attitude was shown by Englishman, John Newton (1788) who was a slaver along the Guinea Coast but then became a vicar in 1764's London. He observed the slavers' attitudes towards some African rulers/traders as, **'... people to be robbed and spoiled, with impunity. Every art is employed to deceive and wrong them'.**

> *... although the Abbraers panyarred the Cormanteen people, yet they dare not sell them for they are all of one country. Quote 16: Richard Thelwall, 1682*

It is significant to remember that, the root cause of African trafficking lay with the invention of "chattel slavery", which was not known by African "collaborators" within the Gold Coast itself. Moreover, Walter Rodney (1966) has shown that the British 'slave trade broke up tribal life and millions of de-tribalised Africans were let loose upon one another'.

> *In procuring slaves from the coast of Africa, many children are stolen privately, wars also are encouraged among the [N]egroes: but all is at a great distance. Many groans arise from dying men, which we hear not. Many cries are uttered by widows and fatherless children. Quote 15: Anthony Benezet: Quakers 1748*

Eurocentrics distort "Africans" complicity to justify their own involvement. Additionally, they projected their own society, racial and cultural arrogances on what they thought they saw. Even English envoy Robert S. Rattray, (1927) said that the **'condition of voluntary servitude was, ... the heritage of every Ashanti'.**

What makes Negroes plenty and gold scarce?

Whites encouraged conflicts by deception, and by favouring one Kingdom against another. This ensured a ready supply of captives. The British already knew that, **"where there's war, there's plenty of Negroes"**, (Kwame Daaku 1970).

The truth is, eurocentric historians deny the significance of the gun-slave cycle, meaning guns, firearms, lead bars and gunpowder were exchanged for captives and goods and vice versa. African historian, Kwame Daaku (1970) highlighted that, guns were 'the greatest single disintegrating force'. African-American Professor of Economics Warren Whatley (2018), has shown that the gun-slave cycle promoted conflict amongst the nations. It was either to raid with guns, or be raided instead.

Eurocentric historians believed middlemen and African elites, dictated nearly all the terms of the British slave trade on an equal partnership! The truth is that, huge differences in power relations existed. Professor F. Ntloedibe (2018) highlighted that, 'historians shift the blame for violent raids from Europeans to Africans'. So that: 'Guilt is taken off Europe for the slave trade and placed on Black people', said eminent African-American Professor of Philosophy, Dr Molefi Asante (2010).

In contrast, a few greedy rulers who were deceived or desired European luxury goods, or who sought to control the British slave trade by collaborating, does not mean they had an equal partnership with white invaders. The British 'used trade as an exterior cover beneath which these violent modes of enslavement operated', concluded Professor F. Ntloedibe (2018). He argued that: 'The role of trade in the enslavement of Africans has been exaggerated', for the benefit of white supremacy.

Image 34: Senior Officer. Note Blunderbuss gun, 1835

It is common practice for these fellows [Europeans] to cheat the Ashantees of nearly one-third of the value of an elephant's tooth … by the Fantee brokers making a bargain with the Europeans for more than they receive in the presence of the Ashantee trader, and the overplus is reserved by the European merchant for the broker, who calls for it the day after…the whites joined with the Fantees in cheating the Ashantees. Quote 17. William Hutton 1821: Voyage to Africa

Thus, **gold became scarce** as people were in **warfare** instead. Even negrophobe Bryan Edwards (1798), said that the 'slave trade encouraged violence in Africa'.

Begun by the British, who had royal permissions, God's blessings (!); royal financing, weapons and soldiers to invade and conquer. Begun by the British who had the *asientos* and whose descendants sustained the trade. Those descendants, evolved into 'a new class of persons'. Identified as, 'mulattos, servants, African assistants … and "merchant princes"', said African historian Kwame Daaku (1970).

Those "new class of persons", aided and abetted the Europeans because, **'where there are oppressors and the oppressed there will be collaborators'**, concluded Dr Molefi Asante (2010).

Who were the Gold Coast Castle Enslaved?

More than thirty slave castles and forts were built by the Europeans along Ghana's coastline. Now these ruins are designated World Heritage Sites by UNESCO and are of Outstanding Universal Value.

African historian Kwame Daaku (1970), identified a "new class of persons" that had evolved. By the end of the 18th century, J. T. Lever (1970) estimated that up to eight hundred mulattoes lived around these castles. Usually, a white European male and an African woman. Angela Sutton (2015) remarked that: 'Offspring of these unions typically ended up in prominent positions in the slave trade, and learnt many European languages'.

Biracial or multiracial people 'were skilled craftsmen including carpenters, bricklayers, sawyers, armourers and canoe men', according to historian, Professor Rebecca Shumway (2014). Her research also found that:

> They moved about freely whilst, tens of thousands of other enslaved African people passed through the same towns in shackles, and suffered in the dungeons of the same forts, on their way to forced passage to the Americas.

Image 35: A Mulatto woman of the Gold Coast: William Hutton. 1821.

Dutch historian Pieter De Marees (1987) described mulatto women as, 'half black, half white, and yellowish, who dress very nicely and are kept by the Portuguese men in the castle as wives'. Natalie Everts (2012) said that 'partners and children of European men could inherit slaves, gold, commodities or real estate'. Until such inheritances were subsequently outlawed, just to prevent Negroes but especially Mulattoes from becoming equal to whites!

Belonging to a group of slavers or merchants, protected multiracial people from being sold and secured their freedom. They were easily recognisable. Professor Pernille Ipsen said that: 'Euro-African women on the Gold Coast ... wore such little bells [that] jingled so much that they could be heard at a great distance'.

> *... they are extremely cleanly, ... at the sea-side, at Cape Coast, washing themselves, which they do every morning early.* Quote 18: William Hutton (1821)

One biracial wealthy male was **Jan Niezer** (1756–1822); trading at Elmina in enslaved people, gold and ivory. J T Lever (1970) accused Niezer of encouraging war between the Ashantis and the Fantes, although this is disputed.

Another wealthy male was, Irishman **Richard Brew** (1725-1776), an English-Fante trader. Together with Captain William Taylor, they shipped captives to Jamaica between 1763-76 (Image 37); mainly from Annamaboe Town, a small fishing village that became one of the most important slaving ports on the Gold Coast. It was, 'well populated besides being very rich in gold, slaves, and corn', according to historian, Professor Trevor R. Getz (2003).

> *Under their cloth they wear a girdle that goes several times round their loins, and forms into a large pad behind, just at the small of their backs, which is called a cankey, and on which they carry their children. This cankey, which has a very un-seemly appearance, possesses the advantage of keeping the cloth loose.* Quote 19: William Hutton (1821

Richard Brew was the Governor of Annamaboe Castle, also known as Castle Brew. He "married" the daughter of **Eno Baise Kurentsi**, a caboceer, meaning a powerful political leader, who was a wealthy Fante slave trader and collaborator. Brew had three biracial children who evolved into an influential elite class of castle enslaved, as shown by Professor Rebecca Shumway (2014).

Who was William Ansah Sessarakoo?

The royal son of a Fante trader, **Eno Baise Kurentsi**, born near Annamaboe on the Gold Coast. William was known as "The Young Prince". In the 15th century, Annamaboe (or Anomabu) evolved from 'a fishing village to a gold-exporting world port in the 17th century to a slave exporting port in the 18th century', according to African-American Professor Ray A. Kea.

The truth is that Europeans fought each other over the Annamaboe trade and derided "Negroes". But despite their contempt, still 'entered into agreements and treaties with these reportedly "savage," and "barbarous" blacks of Africa', wrote Professor Andrew N Wegmann (2014).

Nonetheless, it is said that Eno Baise Kurentsi was adept at playing the Europeans against each other, which gained caboceers, a reputation as "notorious swindlers", (Prof. Rebecca Shumway 2011). William's father, Eno Baise Kurentsi was also called John Corrantee or John Canoe by the English.

Image 36: William Ansah Sessarakoo by Gabriel Mathias (artist) 1749

William Sessarakoo had learnt to speak English residing in Castle Brew as a young child. Born from his chief and royal wife, Eukobah, William was '*diftinguilhed by the quicknefs of his Parts, and the Affability of his Behaviour, as well as by a graceful Deportment, and a very agreeable Perfon*', (no author 1749).

Richard Brew was an Irishman, and officer from the African Company of Merchants, in charge of Castle Brew. His father-in-law (Kurentsi), African "wife", biracial children and extended family, were all involved in human trafficking.

French and English colonists sent his eldest son Lewis Banishee to Paris, and William Ansah Sessarakoo (born 1730) to London. Whilst these merchants sought to win Kurentsi's trading favours by educating his sons, Kurentsi wanted to learn the ways of the Europeans, to outwit them and to maximise his profits, according to the experts.

William Sessarakoo was 'the unfortunate youth [that] had not the least foresight of the impending Evil', (no author 1749). That evil was, the deceitful captain who sold him into enslavement in Barbados in 1744, on the way to be educated in England. The British captain, 'plainly shewed that, in his opinion, all [B]lacks were destined to be slaves'; a typical sentiment. However, until Kurentsi's son was freed, 'he refused to continue trading with any English merchants', explained Professor Vincent Carretta (2012). Thus, the RAC agreed to find him. In return Kurentsi was forced to expel the French.

Royal Africa Company (RAC), 'acted swiftly, dispatched an agent to Barbados to remove Sessarakoo from slavery and bring him to Britain', (Ryan Hanley 2015). In London, William Sessarakoo, together with another African, 'quickly became celebrities', according to Professor Carretta, known everywhere as the Royal Princes, which fed into the "Extraordinary or Exotic Negro" stereotypes. Under the Earl of Halifax's protection, they were dressed lavishly, attended theatres, with fictionalised "noble savage" dramas such as Irish Thomas Southerne's play of "Oroonoko", in London.

The truth is, that **Eno Baise Kurentsi's** family received extensive luxury goods, including arms and ammunition. He may have been one of the 'few greedy rulers', who 'desired European goods [that] outweighed nationalism', according to Professor F. Ntloedibe (2018) or he may have collaborated to control the British slave trade. Furthermore, as some experts believe, the rescuing of William was an RAC "public relations exercise", to show favourable treatment of enslaved people, and to gain trade advantages and favouritism, over the other nations, within the Gold Coast Caboceers.

What is chattel enslavement?

Dr Capt: Willm. Taylor with Richd Brew & Co. Cr

1767 Octob 26 To 43 Men Slaves at 130 5590
To 27 Women Do 110 2970
To 4 Boys Do 110 440
To 2 Do Do 100 200
To 4 Girls Do 80 320
To Ballce Gold ... 8
To 28 Empty heads... 56 — 9584

By 93 hhds Rum ...
By 41 Rolls Tobo ... 984
9589

Errors Excepted ꝑ Richard Brew & Co
Annamaboe 26 October 1767

Mr John Joyce Kingston 12th Augt 1788

Bot of Henry Shewell

Six Negro Slaves as follows
Cato, William, Trouble, Quaco, Jannette
& Holly for transportation £ 315

Recd Payment Same time
Henry Sherrell

N. B. — I have tolled off this day the above Slaves to the sd John Joyce the 1st tole of this Bill of Parcells being one & the same.

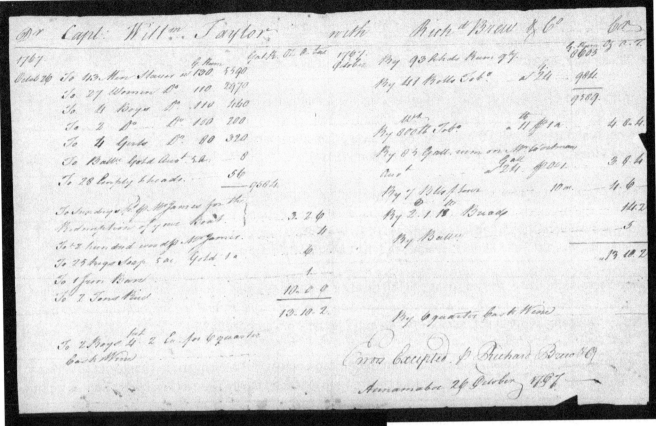

Image 37: Above: ©Capt. William Taylor with Rich'd Brew & Co., Account record by Richard Brew in Annamaboe [Anomabu, Ghana] for Captain William Taylor. Oct. 26, 1710.Slavery Collection, New-York Historical Society, nyhs_sc_b-02_f-18_002:
Image 38 Below: ©Bill of sale for six slaves named Cato, William, Trouble, Quaco, Jannette and Holly, August 12, 1788. New-York Historical Society, Slavery Collection, Series VIII, Subseries 3, John Joyce, Receipts, 1785-1790. nyhs_sc_b-06_f-08_028.1790.

Look at Image 37 above.

1. How many enslaved were brought altogether?
2. Richard Brew wrote this account. True or False.
3. Annamaboe was a British slaving port on the Gold Coast. True or False.
4. Who is this account written for
5. When was it written?
6. How many "iron bars, rum, wine, and soap" were brought?
7. What other information can you find out?

Look at Image 38 carefully.

1. What did John Joyce buy?
2. Where did John Joyce live?
3. When was the Bill of Sale written?
4. Who brought the six enslaved?
5. What can you tell from the names of the enslaved?
6. Name the total price listed?
7. Can you convert that price in today's money?

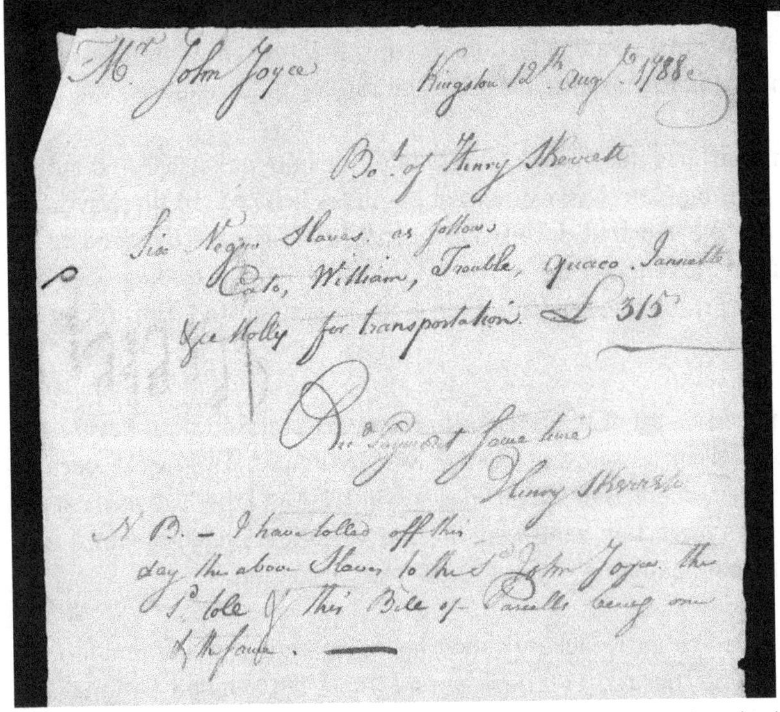

What is chattel enslavement?

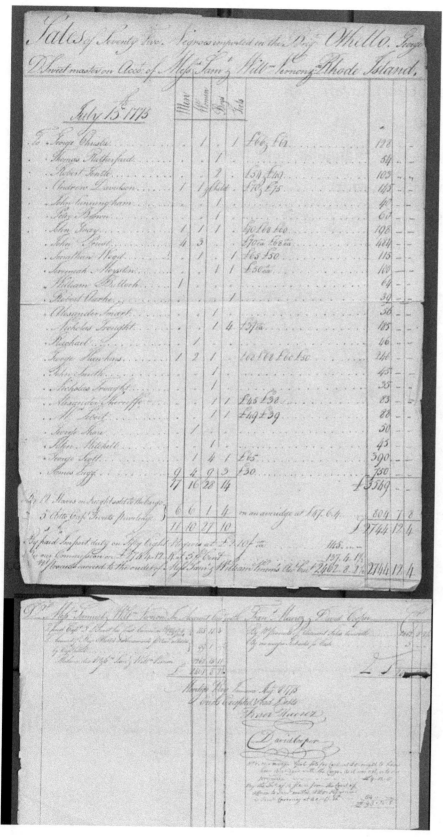

Image 39: Page 1 and 2. Account record for the sale of 75 slaves from the cargo of the Brig Othello, sold by Francis Mairez and David Cooper of Montego Bay, Jamaica, July 15, 1775 on behalf of Samuel and William Vernon [of Newport, Rhode Island]. Includes names of purchasers, price paid, and gender and age of slaves bought.

1. How easy is it to read this document?
2. Is this document a primary or secondary source?
3. Name the slaving ship.
4. Who sold the captives? (Clue: Mairez)
5. What city did the sellers live in?
6. Who were the purchasers?
7. How much import duties were paid for fifty-eight Negroes?
8. How many men, women, girls and boys were sold?
9. What was the total price paid?
10. How much commission was paid?
11. How much import duties were paid?
12. What was the total amount received?

How are these historical documents useful as evidence?

What do these documents reveal about the mentality of the period and of those who made them?

Chapter 5

Image 40: British Battles on Land and Sea: by James Grant, James, 1822-1887: British Library shelfmark: "Digital Store 9504.h.2" Flickr

Why did Oliver Cromwell's Western Design invade in 1655?

Jamaica was: 'Founded in blood when an undisciplined gang of soldiers seized the island from Spain in 1655', wrote renowned historian, Professor Richard S Dunn (1972) because it was 'a perfect base for [buccaneers] to strike against … Cuba, Hispaniola and Central America'.

It was Oliver Cromwell's Western Design, that sent Admiral William Penn and General Robert Venables, under Captain Samuel Hemmings, with troops made up of ruffians and thieves, to conquer, capture and plunder Spanish wealth from Spanish colonies.

So, Cromwell's Western Design had the 'confidence that the English would sweep the Spanish entirely out of the New World', according to historian, Professor Carla Pestana (2005).

Image 41: Painting By Charles Dixon - Saint George in Santa Cruz de Tenerife Anglo Spanish War 1654-1660

Cromwell's Western Design, was a direct confrontation against the Treaty of Tordessilas control of the "New World" and for excluding Britain. Britain had already colonised Barbados in 1627, and wanted to outdo the Spanish and other nations as the biggest Empire, in terms of power, profit and prestige.

But Venables and Penn failed to conquer Hispaniola (Haiti/Dominican Republic). Rather than face humiliation back in Britain, they invaded **Jamaica on 10 May 1655**, at Passage Fort in Kingston's natural harbour; only 611 km from Hispaniola. During this invasion, the Spanish 'freed their slaves, and asked them to help them fight the British', according to eminent anthropologist Kenneth Bilby (2006), but many also escaped to the mountains.

> *… the English troops were slayne by a handfull of cowardly mulatoes and Negroes.*
> Quote 20: [Gregory Butler] to General Disbrowe, [1655]

Those who escaped became the early Maroons, 'said to be about 1,500', according to Bryan Edwards (1798), a slaver and politician. They were never part of British enslavement. In the following centuries, more fugitives joined them in the mountains. Using their intelligence and guerrilla tactics, these early Maroons became the sharpest thorns in the British Colony's plans.

Spain attempted to retake Jamaica in 1657 and 1658. British formal possession took another five years. Hostilities between Spain and Britain, subsided upon the 1670 Treaty of Madrid. Subsequent centuries saw Britain create 'an agricultural economy based on slave labour in support of England's Industrial Revolution', argued Sandra W Meditz, Library Of Congress (1989). One of the first British institutions transferred to Jamaica was London's Westminster Parliament, called **The Jamaican Assembly**. Elected for and by elite white males who were slavers, politicians, merchants, and professionals.

The Royal Africa Company (RAC) was set up and funded by King Charles II, Duke of York and investors in the City of London. The British royal family and financiers invested in this company, which took an average of 1120 Gold Coast captives to Jamaica each year, rising to more than 2700 per annum. 'Between 1672 and 1713 the RAC transported some 100,000 enslaved Africans across the Atlantic', according to historian, Professor Robin Blackburn (1997) before the *Asiento de Negroes.* The British had expanded exponentially what the Spanish had started.

Who won the battle of Rio Nuevo?

The British. The battle was Spain's last attempt to take back Jamaica, near the river Rio Nuevo on the north coast in St Mary's parish, where there are a 'complex of Taíno sites', according to JHNT (2011), now in ruins.

1655: The year Cromwell's soldiers invaded and captured Jamaica from the Spanish. Africans and Taínos had escaped and evolved into the early Maroons; Juan de Bolas (Lubolo is his African name) of St Catherine Mountains; Juan de Serras of Cockpit Country; African and Taínos cohabited in the eastern Blue Mountains and another group in the west.

1657: Jamaica's location was the easiest access to the Spanish markets of Cartagena, Havana, Vera Cruz and Porto Bello. Hence, the Spanish fought to keep Jamaica but they failed in the Battle of Las Chorreras (Ocho Rios).

1658: The Spanish failed again to reclaim Jamaica at Rio Nuevo.

1660: The British fought both the Spanish loyalists and the Maroons until the Spanish were finally defeated. Then the Spanish fled to Cuba.

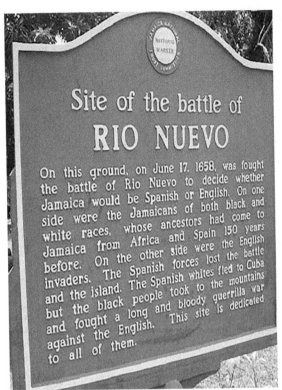

Image 42: The Rio Nuevo Memorial. Jamaican National Heritage Site and Rio Nuevo Taíno Site

1662: Thousands of English white convicted criminals landed to make their fortunes. Poor Scottish and Irish followed, as indentured labourers; Portuguese-Spanish Jews arrived, fleeing persecution.

1670: Formal British colony under the Treaty of Madrid which ended the continuous warfare between England and Spain. Subsequently, whites made tremendous fortunes because, as Professor James Walvin (2000) has shown, Jamaican land was theirs by "right of conquest", guaranteeing the inheritance of intergenerational wealth, but the exact parallel opposite for African or Indian peoples. Captain Samuel Hemmings, of the Penn and Venables British forces, took a 2500-acre parcel of land, which included the earlier Spanish **Seville La Nueva site**, now called Seville Heritage Park, and subsequently made fortunes for their descendants.

After 1662, all [those] born in Jamaica are subjects of England

1724: Captain Samuel Hemming's son, also named Samuel Hemmings (Junior), was left £2000 and land to his daughter Elizabeth. His other son, Richard, together with Samuel Junior, were left a cow pen called Little Thickets, "to build upon it a sugar mill and to settle it with at least 50 working slaves". By 1754 Richard Hemming owned 2296 acres of St Ann's land and 500 acres in St James's parish, (Legacies of British Slavery).

1755: Captain Samuel Hemmings also left to his son, Samuel (Junior), his St Ann's Seville Estate and thousands of pounds for all of his grandchildren's education and support. By 1756, 315 enslaved Africans worked at this estate, valued at £12,935, (Legacies of British Slavery).

Since 2009, the Nuevo battle site is a Heritage Park, donated to the Jamaican National Heritage Trust by the owners, the infamous sugar tycoons, the **Beckford family of slavers.** They owned over seventeen plantations; five livestock pens and 1,669 enslaved in 1735. The Beckfords were awarded £12,803 reparations after abolition as shown by Sidney Blackmore (2018) of the English Beckford Society. Not only did the enslaved labourers received nothing, but they were unable to pass on any intergenerational wealth or land, the legacy of which, has led to endemic poverty and sufferation for the masses.

Who were the real pirates of Port Royal?

Taíno Indians used Port Royal as a fishing camp. Later, the Spanish used it 'for cleaning, refitting and caulking of their sailing vessels', noted JNHT (2011). Port Royal was the first major British settlement before it sunk into the Caribbean Sea. Now Port Royal has been immortalised in the *Pirates of the Caribbean* films. Professor Richard S Dunn, (1972) described it as a 'handsome, wealthy, and surprisingly cosmopolitan place, altogether a colourful little city'. A few pirates were:

Sir Henry Morgan (Welsh) who ran the buccaneer fleets. Morgan, with hundreds of crewmen, destroyed Spanish towns on behalf of the British. With his wealth, he brought sugar plantations and hundreds of enslaved people. He was knighted in 1674 and became Governor of Jamaica. His name lives on, as a Captain Morgan label on rum bottles.

Blackbeard (English) became legendary of all pirates with his long-plaited hair and beard. His real name was said to be Edward Teach or Thache. Born about 1680, paid as a privateer by the British to steal and plunder from Spanish and French enemy ships and towns until the British changed tactics and hanged him in 1718.

Calico Jack Rackham (English) was a famous pirate because two women pirates called **Mary Read** and **Anne Bonny**, were dressed as men and fought alongside Calico. He was also famous for wearing flamboyant colourful Indian Calico clothes, as well as

Image 43: Above: Ann Bonny and Mary Read convicted of Piracy Nov. 28th 1720. Below: Fort Charles. Giddy House in Port Royal, built in 1880 JNHT (2011)

flying his Jolly Roger pirate flag. In 1720, Rackham was caught at a Negril rum punch party, hanged in an iron cage and suspended on an islet, later called Rackham's Cay. Both women were pregnant and imprisoned but then freed.

Black Caesar (African) was a successful pirate. Originally captured by slavers from Africa, but escaped during a shipwreck near Florida. 'He eventually joined Blackbeard's crew. "60 of Blackbeard's crew of 100 [pirates] were black", at one time in 1718', claimed historian Marcus Rediker (2004). However, eurocentric historians believe Black Caesar is a legend, because "Caesar", was an unidentifiable name given to any enslaved person.

1692 Earthquake sank the 'wickedest and richest city in the world' into Kingston's harbour. Called the 'Sodom and Gomorrah of the world'; due to its lawlessness, debauchery, smuggling, and wealth that was begun by the British who paid pirates to plunder from Spanish and French ships and towns. About 600-700 captives died that day.

1907 Earthquake further damaged Kingston and Port Royal. The Royal Artillery House, built in 1880, remains partially sunk; nicknamed the "Giddy House". A 'monument over the graves' of where the '501 unidentified victims of this natural disaster were buried', (JHNT 2011), was erected in 1909.

Today, Port Royal is a small coastal fishing village with half the city still undersea. It is a potential World Heritage Site, historic town and a haven for underwater treasure seekers. The truth is that Jamaican pirates are the, 'objects of popular fascination, glamorisation and nostalgia', as shown by Professor Erin Mackie's 2005 research. She believes that they are all part of Jamaica's subcultures, because pirates involve masculine fantasies of outlaw glamour including complicity with the authorities; similar to another Jamaican subculture, that of the Maroons.

What is the Irish myth?

That they were enslaved as **"Black men in white skins"**! But: 'Servants received cost of their passage and food, clothing, and shelter ... in return for up to seven years of contracted labour', said Sir Hilary Beckles, an eminent Barbadian Professor. Chattel enslavement had no end but white skins knew when their freedom ended.

Image 44: Illustration from James Mursell Phillippo's 'Jamaica: Its Past and Present State,' depicting the village of Sligoville. 1843

The British colonial experience began in Ireland. 17th century Irish governors had, 'orders to arrest ... all wanderers, men and women and such other Irish', as well as 'all children ... in hospitals or workhouses, all prisoners ... to be transported to the West Indies', said Joseph Williams, (1932), a Jesuit priest. The English saw Irish Catholics as enemies, 'stereotyped as disobedient, lazy, and aggressive', similar to the stereotypes of Africans. But, Frederick Douglass (1850), a well-known US Black abolitionist in England and Ireland, argued that: 'The Irishman may be poor but he is not a slave. He may be in rags but he is not a slave .... The Irishman has not only the liberty to emigrate from his country but he has liberty at home. He can write, speak, and co-operate for the attainment of his rights ... ', (Douglas).

> INDENTURE AGREEMENT
> PATRICK BURKE 1739 London
> *Be it remember'd that Patrick Burke of Dublin in the Kingdom of Ireland, Bookkeeper his Father and Mother being dead, did by Indenture bearing like Date herewith, agree to serve Joseph Whilton of London Chapman, or his assigns four years in Jamaica In the Employment of a Bookkeeper at 30 li [i.e., £30] per annum Current Money of Jamaica.* Quote 21: Jamaican Family Search

By 1835, the first free village was named Sligoville (in St Catherine), after Irishman, Howe Peter Browne, the 2nd Marquis of Sligo (a town in Ireland), who became Governor of Jamaica (1834-6). Freed people had nowhere to live. Slavers refused to rent to former captives, others charged high rents or evicted them or charged children rent. Thus Englishman, Baptist Reverend James Phillippo brought land and divided it into plots for freed people to live somewhere. Together, Phillipo and Sligo built a school and a church and renamed the area, Sligoville.

By 1844, over one hundred free villages were modelled on Sligoville. But the truth is, they were not free. £3 was paid for their ¼ acre. Furthermore, "free" villages, were opportunities to transform former captives into white Victorian British; learning gendered roles where women became the property of husbands instead of slavers; learning British education that had little to do with their environment or situation, and learning about the preservation of white supremacy within their "Christian" churches. Conversely most former enslaved, repurposed and redefined these norms as they saw fit.

Nonetheless, Sligoville is significant because many inhabitants are, 'direct descendants of the freed slaves', according to JIS (Rochelle Williams 2018) and that: 'Sligoville is the birthplace of the Rastafarian movement, with the first Rastafarian village named Pinnacle established there in 1940'. Despite historians' views that the Marquis of Sligo "detested slavery", and "set his own captives free from apprenticeships", he was awarded £3221 13 shillings 11d (pence) reparations for Kelly's Pen and £2,304 15 shillings 2d (pence) for Cocoa Kelly Walk estates, according to the Legacies of British Slavery. This Irish slave-owning family, reached the height of Ireland's aristocracy due to their wealth made from African enslavement and their tropical goods. The truth is that: 'The Irish were not slaves in the way that Africans in the Caribbean were', explained Jamaican Lecturer, Robert Johnson (2018).

Irishmen were the colonised and colonisers, as well as the oppressed and oppressors.

What, to enslaved people, is the "triangular slave trade"?

The first part of the British slave trade, involved deceit, trickery and kidnapping people from the Gold Coast. Captives were locked up in dungeons in the "castles", whilst waiting for vessels to fill up; attended by the castle enslaved.

Professor Dr Molefi Asante (2005) highlighted that, 'accounts of resistance solidified a record of African rebellion in the Middle Passage'. The constant threat of enslaved mutinies and African resistors shaped history because insurance products and policies forced costs up (Dr Asante).

The second part, involved the tight packing of people on slaving vessels. Then sailing on the graveyard that is the Atlantic Ocean. The truth is, that there was nothing *"middle" about the transportation of millions of Africans from the Gold Coast for Africans.*

As historian, Professor Marcus Rediker (2004) has shown, 'slave ships were simultaneously mobile war machines, prisons, and floating factories'. Despite this, even in cramped spaces, resistances included onboard insurrections and mass suicides (Dr Asante 2005). Eurocentric historians focused on conditions of death, this ignored the fact that, during the middle passage, survivors may have given **'birth to a new African person'**, revealed Dr Asante (2005).

The third part of the British slave trade involved arrival in Jamaica. Then Africans were branded, renamed, inspected, separated and put up for auctions at scramble or private sales. But this was not the end of the "triangle" for Africans. Those who stayed in Jamaican were "seasoned" and transported to main towns or rural interiors. As Jamaica was a major trans-shipment centre, over 200,000 captives were shipped onwards, undertaking further journeys, or to other colonies. Moreover, the truth is that the British continued in human trafficking, even though they had outlawed the trade and enslavement in 1807 and the 1830s.

The NLJ (n.d.) estimated that **600,000** Africans were sent to Jamaica between 1533 and 1807. Professor Trevor Burnard Director from The Wilberforce Institute (2020) estimated that, 'nearly **900,000** Africans landed at Kingston's waterfront'. There were no listed British arrivals before 1651. But, **1,500** was calculated when the Spanish occupied the island by Bryan Edwards (1798), who was a white Jamaican slaver, historian and Member of England's Westminster Parliament.

After the 1807 Abolition Act and up to 1850, the Voyages Database adds another **6,430** from Britain. Thus, the Act was worthless because Britain continued to participate in the buying and selling of Gold Coast Africans after 1807. Including the other nations of European slavers; Spain, Portugal, Netherlands, USA, France and Denmark, adds another **25,069** between 1601-1850. With rampant smuggling, over one million Africans landed in Jamaica; significantly higher than all other Caribbean islands combined; some carried by the infamous Liverpool, UK ships, such as the *Zong* and *Brookes*.

According to Encyclopedia Britannica: 'Jamaica became one of the world's busiest slave markets, with a thriving smuggling trade to Spanish America'. Approximately, **1,182,625** Africans landed in Jamaica between 1651 and 1850. Historian, Madeleine Burnside (1997) remarked that, 'the reckoning in human lives was staggering, almost incomprehensible'. For Britons, the "triangular slave trade" was divided into three organisational business parts. The truth is, the journey was one long continuous experience of human degradation; **from capture to captive to chattel.** Therefore, what to the enslaved is the triangular nature of the British slave trade?

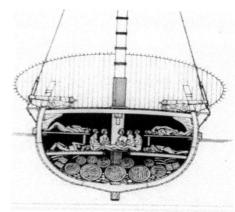

	British Caribbean
	Jamaica
1651-1700	116,638
1701-1750	387,181
1751-1800	602,854
1801-1850	75,952
Totals	1,182,625

Image 45: Above Cross section Reconstruction of the English slaver, Henrietta Marie ship to Jamaica 1699-1700. Below. Number of captives that landed in Jamaica from Slave Voyages.org

How white men get away with murder!

Insurance fraud! A Liverpool slaving vessel, called *Zong*, licensed to carry 292 Africans, departed for Jamaica in September 1781 from the Gold Coast, arriving at Black River, St Elizabeth's parish in December. Originally named *Zorgue*, it stopped in São Tomé to collect more Africans. A total of 442 captives were onboard. Before arrival, somewhere in the Atlantic Ocean, **133 captives were deliberately thrown overboard for insurance money.**

Owners of the *Zong* slaving vessel were brothers William and James Gregson. They were also, Lord Mayors of Liverpool (UK). Luke Collingwood was the captain. During the Atlantic crossing, sixty enslaved had already died; but veering off course caused Captain Collingwood to deliberately throw 133 captives overboard. Eurocentrics believed that it was a sacrifice to save the remaining captives and crew due to low supplies on board.

Image 46: Plaque to honour Zong victims in Black River, Jamaica

Zong (renamed *The Richard*) returned to England in 1782. Brothers Gregson claimed in court, on their insurance and won damages because Africans were "property"! But the insurers did not want to pay out. Upon investigation, the insurers found that their claim was fraudulent. The ship had arrived in Black River with 420 gallons of water. Therefore, the lack of supplies were not true. The truth is that:

> *This was an insurance scam of monstrous proportions, in which the Africans had been murdered so that the ship's owners could claim compensation for their loss.*
> Quote 22: Granville Sharp's Letter re Zong incident 23 May 1783

- those chosen for deliberate drowning were already seriously ill
- sick captives would fetch nothing in the slavers' market; known as "refuse slaves"

Hence, Lord Chief Justice Mansfield's comment during the High Court appeal in May 1783, that throwing captives overboard was, **'exactly the same as throwing horses'**! Because the all-encompassing attitudes of whites towards Black people, was shown by the Governor of Jamaica who commented that:

> It is treason in Jamaica to talk of a Negro as a freeman. The black and coloured population are viewed by the white inhabitants as little more than semi-human, for the most part a kind of intermediate race, possessing indeed the form of man, but none of his finer attributes, (Lord Sligo, Howe Peter Browne).

However, Granville Sharp, a British abolitionist, demanded that murder charges must be brought against the crew. He argued that 'evil [murder] cannot be justified by necessity [low supplies]', according to Professor Tim Armstrong (2004), but the insurers still won and did not have to pay insurance.

Yet, there were no punishments. **The crew and owners got away with murder.** The only significant interest for whites, centered on the legal point of claiming on insurances for "chattels". The truth is that the foundation of "Lloyd's of London"; the "Royal & Sun Alliance", and so on, built their companies by insuring such vessels and goods for the British slave trade.

Additionally, for every ten slaving ships, there was one enslaved rebellion, according to the experts, which increased slavers' insurance and other costs. The constant threat of an enslaved mutiny meant slavers refined their Middle Passage methods and maritime laws to bring even greater profits and to defend against rebellions, as the centuries progressed.

British professor and eminent historian James Walvin (2011) said that: 'The Zong's legacy was clear to white people that it exposed the sufferings endured by millions of Africans on slave ships', and that the, 'essential truth is that the slave system was rotten to the core'. However, such treatment was nothing new to "New Negroes" who told their own tales as survivors, and of those thrown overboard, called "refuse slaves", as regular occurrences.

What was the Jamaican Scramble Sale?

Between 1790–1795, most of the 103,560 captives from 373 voyages were forcibly taken to Kingston harbour, as shown by Professor Kenneth Morgan (2016), a British historian.

18th century, Scottish John Tailyour, (Taylor) sold 17,295 captives on 54 British vessels; providing credit for slavers' voyages. He became immensely wealthy, said Professor Morgan, from commissions on each sale when he delivered.

Even though John Taylor said that Negroes, 'differ only from Bruite beast only by their shape and speech', he had four Biracial children with a Jamaican "partner". He retired in Scotland with his English wife and left nearly £100,000 at his death in 1816. Both John Taylor and JB Moreton (1793) advertised Scramble Sales. One such sale was from the *Alert* ship,(Image 47 above).

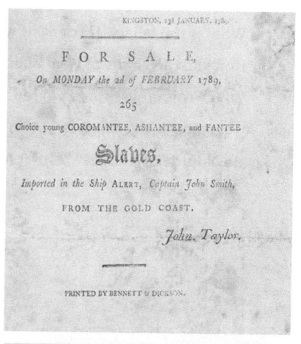

- prime captives kept on board until the day of the sale
- captives were made to "exercise". Any observer would misconstrue those sightings as "happy, singing and dancing Negroes on deck"!
- kept 'dead bodies' .... 'in the hold until night', and then 'given to the sharks, which devour them in a trice'. In case gossip about sickly Negroes ruined their profits.
- separated into healthy, ill and refuse slaves.
- separated into privilege men, cargo men, privilege men-boys, men-boys, boys, and similar for females.
- rich buyers had private viewings and brought the healthiest and most expensive captives first.
- after primes were sold, other buyers 'simultaneously rushed into the yard or top deck of the ship ... and seized whoever was available'. They **pick and choose them like manner as if sheep or oxen; and grabble, grasp and jostle each other to get the best'**, wrote Moreton. This was the **Scramble Sale.**
- captives were separated from their families and shipmates; branded with the owner's initials or sold onwards. Reverend W. J. Gardner (1873) a missionary in Jamaica, wrote that , 'the [N]egro, whether born or acclimatised in a mountain or lowland district, suffered when removed from one to the other'. Slavers deliberately broke up families, friends or ethnic groups or "ship-mates" to emphasise the chattel position of captives.

Guyanese-British Professor David Dabydeen of Warwick University said: 'It was a nasty unimaginable way of treating people as goods, with no sense of humanity'.

Image 47: Above: ©A handbill advertising the sale of the Alert's captive Africans 1789. John Tailyour to Simon Taylor in Simon Taylor Papers. Jamaica c 1765-1848. Senate House Library. Below: Slavers separate families, friends, shipmates and send them to various plantations, towns or other countries.

> ... *if they are afflicted with any infirmity, or are deformed, or have bad eyes or teeth; if they are lame, or weak in the joints, or distorted in the back, or of a slender make, or are narrow in the chest; in short, if they have been, or are afflicted in any manner, so as to render them incapable of much labour ...they are rejected.* Quote 23: Alexander Falconbridge (1788)

Chapter 6

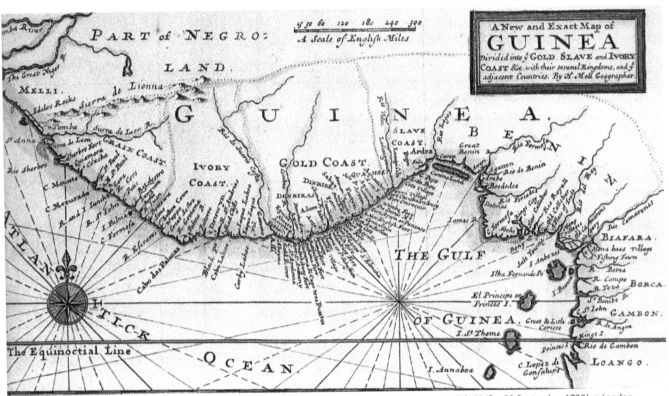

Image 48: HISTORIC MAP OF THE COAST OF WEST AFRICA, THEN CALLED "GUINEA", c. 1725 by Herman Moll (1654? – 22 September 1732), a London cartographer, engraver, and publisher.

Notes: "Guinea Street" in Bristol, UK, is named after the West Coast of Africa. A pub at the end of that street is called "The Golden Guinea". This is one area where many slavers had residences.

British money, used to be called the "Guinea". Also named after the coast of West Africa. The British Guinea coins were issued from 1663 onwards by the Royal Africa Company (RAC) with an elephant on the reverse. The Guinea was the most valuable form of British currency, before being replaced by the pound note and then the pound coin.

What is the fallacy of scientific racism?

Scientific racism is **bad science** developed by eurocentrics and white supremacists to **justify** enslavement; to **defend** colonialism that evolved into **race** and **racism**. Yet, there is 'no valid religious and cultural basis for racial hierarchy, and no biological or genetic piece of knowledge, that could establish racial distinctions among human beings', wrote Jorge L. Giovannetti (2006) a Professor of Sociology. Remember that racism is a system of advantage based on skin colour and unequal power relationships that only benefits whites. Scientific racism, therefore, is a method to justify their privileges.

The truth is that, acting and thinking as though there were specific "races", assumes that "race" does exist as a religious, biological, or genetic fact. 'Racism is the consequence of a prefabricated 'myth of race'; which was used to allow atrocities to be committed throughout the slave trade and slavery', as shown by Professors Audrey Smedley and others (2020).

These following "scientists", divided people into a hierarchy of races:

1. Botanist, Carl Linnaeus published Systema Naturae in 1759
2. German anthropologist, Johann Blumenbach published Crania Germanica in 1795
3. Samuel Morton published Crania Aegyptiaca 1844, Catalogue of Skulls of Man, 1849.
4. Ernst Haeckel, a German Darwin: Evolution of Man 1867, History of Creation, 1887; used by Nazi eugenicists.

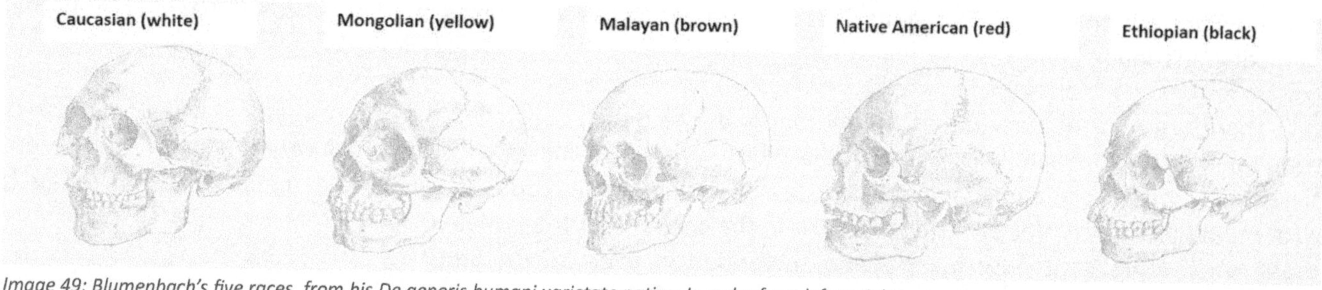

Caucasian (white)	Mongolian (yellow)	Malayan (brown)	Native American (red)	Ethiopian (black)

Image 49: Blumenbach's five races, from his De generis humani varietate nativa: In order from left to right.

Samuel Morton believed that Caucasian (white) skulls were superior to Ethiopian (Black), because Black people had smaller skulls and therefore less intelligence! White supremacists stated scientific racist ideas as "facts" which, in modern times, have been totally disproven. But these myths still remain because the 'starkly racial character', of the British slave trade, 'was more profoundly oppressive and more socially divisive than Graeco-Roman slavery or medieval serfdom', claimed historian, Professor Richard S Dunn (1972). Meaning that **chattel enslavement rose to new heights of dehumanisation than ancient or medieval slavery.**

Racial categories have no biological basis

'One of the widest spread and most damaging legacies of the British slave trade and enslavement is racism, institutionalised, cultural and structural, which has repercussions on all continents', wrote UNESCO (2021) and that: 'Diasporic Africans continue to experience the legacies of racism in many different guises today'. But the exact opposite allows the privileges associated with whites and whiteness, regardless of their individual class or gender.

University of Pennsylvania argued that, 'the biggest fault in Morton's research may lie in that he didn't collect data on body size ... [because] brain size correlates to body size'. Yet the truth is, the "biggest fault", is spreading as scientific fact that Black people had smaller skulls and therefore less intelligence as justification for Black people as "incapable of being educated" and "natural slaves".

The truth is that, together with religious fallacies, "scientific racism" was given "respectability" through these and other so-called "scientists". Heathens, must be "controlled, converted or eliminated" (Gallagher 2007) because they are not white nor Christian. One such religious fallacy was the "Curse of Ham" that sanctified enslavement as divinely decreed.

How did the curses of Ham affect African peoples?

Missionaries taught enslaved people that Christians must **endure suffering** and **obey their masters,** because they were "cursed", e.g., destined to be "natural slaves". The truth is, that one specific Bible verse was wrongly interpreted, misused, and abused (amongst many others). Genesis 9.18-27 'has arguably been the most widespread justification for condemning dark skinned peoples to slavery', concluded Professor Benjamin Braude (2011). This is called, the *Curse of Ham*:

Noah and his three sons Shem, Ham, and Japheth, left the ark following the flood
- Ham, saw his father whilst drunk, without clothes and mocked him.
- Noah cursed Ham for his behaviour and thus, he "turned Black". (Remember that "Black" became associated with all things sinful, danger, inferior and so on).
- Ham's son, Canaan, was cursed to be the servants of Shem and Japheth.
- As these ancient peoples dispersed over the world after the flood
  o Shem's descendants were "Yellow or Red" and populated Asia
  o Japheth's descendants were "White" and populated Europe
  o Ham's descendants, Canaan, had dual curses of "Blackness and slavery" and populated Africa. Blackness was divine creation or being "blackened" as punishment by the scorching sun. All constituted marks of perpetual degradation.

> Colonel William Byrd's Letter to the Earl of Egmont, 1736
> *We have already at least 10,000 Men of these descendants of Ham fit to bear Arms ...* Quote 24: Elizabeth Donnan 1833-1955

Yet, '**there are no anti-black or racist sentiments in the Bible**', concluded history Professor David Goldenberg's wide-ranging 2009 research. 'Nowhere in the Bible is the belief that Black skin colour equals a life of oppression, slavery or servitude', he argued. Emeritus Professor, Dean A. Miller 2005 review of Professor Goldenberg's research wrote that, 'distortion of the text does not lie in the text, but in the minds of those who would try to use it, and who succeeded in using it, for other purposes'. Accordingly, the truth is:

1. God blessed all Noah's sons, after the mocking event, in Genesis.
2. Noah and his family were not racially described in the Bible.
3. It was Noah who cursed Canaan, not God.
4. Old Testament curses were lifted by Jesus's death in the New Testament.
5. Semitic/Hebrew misinterpretations of "Ham" to mean "hot, dark or black".
6. Continents were not in the formations as they are now
7. Whiteness was *not* "blessed with divine authority" in Japheth (racial hierarchy).

The Bible also talks about freedom, equality and justice in Exodus, Leviticus and Deuteronomy

However, if Ham "turned Black", and if Shem and Japheth had the same parents as Ham, then the whole earth would have been populated with Black people, as they dispersed. Evidence by scientist, Dr Anders Bergström's original research in 2021, has shown that: 'Modern humans originated in Africa within the past 300,000 years' or 200,000 years according to NHM, (UK). Hence, our human race is originally an African one. Modern humans completed migration to all continents, except Antarctica, between 50,000-10,000 BCE. The NHM said that, 'lighter skin pigmentation in Europe over the last 9,000 years, ... related to an increased need for UV induced vitamin D synthesis in the skin'. Nonetheless, racist misuse of biblical texts demonstrated how far whites went, to justify chattel enslavement.

Captives were not allowed to be literate. Ignorance led to some believing in these distortions. Today, Christian obedience to the "white God" has left Jamaica with more "churches" per square mile than any other country in the world! Ultimately, it was the Black "Christians" who synthesised white Christianity with African cosmologies (traditional explanations about the universe and meanings of life). They proved to be the sharpest thorns in the British colony plans for Jamaica. In fact, in 1824 prominent Methodist Richard Watson puts it perfectly when he said that, '**the only curse under which the African continent then suffered, was the curse of European exploitation**'!

Which colour was three degrees removed from African?

'In Jamaica, [B]lacks outnumbered whites between 10:1 and 15:1', according to Jamaican Professor, Orlando Patterson (1973). So, whites lived in perpetual fear and threat of uprisings. But violence was not enough to control captives. It was better to 'persuade the [B]lack man to accept the allegation of his own inferiority', wrote E.T. Thompson (1975); because

- 'slavery was the ultimate race-making institution', argued Haitian Professor Michel-Rolph Trouillot (1998)
- 'physical traits led to the creation of what we now call race and racism', wrote Dr James A Delle (2009)
- 'racism conveniently justified ... forced black labour', concluded Professor Richard S Dunn (1972)
  Thus, racism is a "white problem", that negatively affects the life chances of anybody who is not "white".

Additionally, the minority of whites needed **allies.** Achieved in law by three generations removed from an African ancestor. Giving legal "white" status, meant "the rights and privileges of Englishmen, born of white ancestors". It was called, the **Private Acts of the Assembly of Jamaica 1733.**

Legal Status	Parent Male	Parent Female	Child Status
White	White	Quintroon	Octroroon
	White	Mustifino	Quintroon
	White	Mustee	Mustifino
	White	Quadroon	Mustee
Enslaved/	White	Mulatto	Quadroon
Coloureds	White	Negro	Mulatto
Enslaved /	Mulatto	Negro	Sambo
Free Blacks	Negro	Negro	Negro

Arnold Sio (1976) Race, Colour, and Miscegenation: The Free Coloured of Jamaica and Barbados. Caribbean Studies, 16(1), 5-21

This Act indirectly encouraged women to have lighter skinned children to bring them closer to legal whiteness. Professor Michael Craton (1997) said that the reverse was true for men. 'The lighter his colour, the less likely was he to father children lighter than himself, or even of his own colour'.

Professor Arnold Sio (1976) has shown that, in manumission cases, whites preferred to free:

- mulattoes (one black and one white parent or two mulattoes) rather than African peoples.
- octoroons were legal whites (one African great-grandparent and 7 white great grandparents – 1/8th African).
- mustees (1/8th African - from Spanish mestizo, - Negro and Indian) were lighter and so had more privileges.
- mustifinoes (1/16th), more prestige than mustees and quadroons (one African and three white grandparents).

The "legal whites" or "whites-by-law", included "poor whites," and "free browns" or "coloureds", who viewed themselves as superior; pretentious; showing contempt for fellow Africans as Tekla Ali Johnson (2004) has shown. Started and reinforced by whites. The truth is, 'the majority of mixed-race' or 'coloureds', remained enslaved and shared a common identity with the black majority', according to Black British Liverpool-born Professor, Stephen Small (1994). He said that: **'In Jamaica in 1825, 400 of the free people of mixed-race were rich, 5,500 were in fair circumstances and 22,900 were absolutely poor'**. Therefore, whites may have exaggerated the advantages of lighter skin to divide and control.

The harshness of chattel enslavement meant some Africans accepted the allegations of their own inferiorities. Moreover, the lighter the skin, the better the social position, attractiveness and desirability of Black people in white eyes; internalised by some Black people. Thus, Captain Bedford Pim (1866), an English barrister and British Royal Navy officer said: 'The [N]egro will obey a white man more readily than a mulatto, and a mulatto rather than one of his own colour'. The result of these laws led to a three-tiered colour system of whites, browns and Black people that correlated with class hierarchies.

These issues evolved into darker-skinned people "skin bleaching". "Bleachers" believed lighter skins would enhance their economic, social life choices and opportunities, despite the adverse health risks. Dr Christopher Charles (2011) from UWI highlighted that, 'skin bleaching is a global phenomenon driven by colourism which is an offshoot of racism', and that it, 'links Jamaica's past and present'.

In fact, a popular statement that used to be said by Jamaicans was: **If you're white you're alright, if you're brown, stick around, if you're black get back.**

How did African captives obtain manumission?

Manumission involved slavers setting the enslaved person free. This involved transfers of written documents as deeds, that were witnessed, sealed and registered, with compensation for loss of "property". Prof. David B. Ryden's research (2018), showed that 460 people were freed between 1772 and 1774. Professor, Stephen Small (1994) confirmed that there were 'about 500 manumissions each year', who were mostly 'mixed-race'. Other methods for gaining freedom were:

Religion: For better lives, some Black people pretended to worship the "white man's god" to gain access to the "white man's power".

Buying own freedom: Only four of the 317 deeds showed a captive purchasing his or her own freedom, (Professor Ryden 2018).

Informers: Alerting on conspiracies led to "freedom" as in Jack's case (Quote 25). In St Thomas's parish, Sambo, a free Negro became an informer; his wife and seven children were freed for 'great service against the rebellious and runaway Negroes', (Private Acts of the Assembly of Jamaica 1733).

Jack

Whereas a [N]egro man named Jack, the property of Peter Thomas, of the parish of St. Mary, planter, has been very instrumental in the discovery of rebellious conspiracies and was extremely active in suppressing the late rebellion in the said parish: ... rewarded for such fidelity and services to the public ... is hereby manumitted and set free ... on the first day of May ... during his life pay him the sum of £5 as a reward. Quote 25: Acts of Assembly. 19th December 1761

Relatives: Peter Furnell's four-year-old son, Richard, was given the, 'same rights and privileges with English subjects born of white parents'. His mother was a free Negro. After 1774, slavers paid a £5 annual fee to stop freed people from becoming "great nuisances". This ruling kept many in bondage who might have otherwise been freed.

Black into White: As chattel enslavement was hereditary, it took three generations to produce a white person from African ancestors to gain, 'full entry into the white man's world', (Bryan Edwards 1798), notably a "quadroon". In 1787 Penelope Brewer a free mulatto woman, had two quadroon children, Robert and Helen, who were entitled to the same privileges as English subjects, born of white parents; '... free from all manner of Slavery and Bondage whatsoever', said the Acts of the Assembly. Hence today, many modern people who look white, have African ancestors. This is confirmed by Dr Adam Rutherford (2020), a geneticist and BBC presenter who said that: **'Racial purity is pure fantasy. For humans, there are no pure bloods'**, and that: 'Every racist has African, Indian, East Asian ancestors, as well as everyone else'.

White fathers: James Wedderburn, wealthy slaver of Westmoreland, said in his 1797 will: 'I give devise and bequeath unto a mulatto child, daughter of my [N]egro wench named Fanny, four new [N]egroes ... Fanny be made free and ... allowed £10 currency p/a during her natural life', according to Legacies of British Slavery.

Towns v. Rural: More enslaved in towns such as Kingston or Port Royal, were manumitted than those in rural regions especially those located on interior plantations. By the second or third generations, Professor Ryden (2018) found that, '98 percent of the manumitted people ... were freed between 1770 and 1774', in towns.

Professor Maria A. Bollettino (2020) calculated that, '... free people of colour steadily increased from just over 1000 in 1730 to more than 3400 by 1762, and 7065 by 1788'. Still, freed people also faced restrictive laws. The truth is that, '... families of mulattoes are left upon the estates by successive white overseers and bookkeepers who consign their children to slavery, with as much indifference as with his old shoes', anonymously written (1790 Marly).

The legacy of this, is that if African peoples "looked white enough", they could enter the "white world" of opportunities, choices and privileges but yet, still with restrictions. Those restrictions today result in structural and institutional racism that excluded Black people from "white" professions, "white" organisations, "white" politics and "white" businesses.

How did "Slave Codes" restrict African captives?

The first Jamaican Slave Code was enacted in 1664, modified in 1684 and 1696. The 1696 Codes were adopted from the 1661 Barbados Codes called: *An Act for Better Ordering and Governing of Negroes*. It referred to Negroes as, 'a heathenish, brutish and an uncertaine, dangerous kinde of people'.

"Slave Codes" restricted the behaviours of captives. But enforcing them in towns (Kingston, Port Royal, Montego Bay, Spanish Town etc), or on rural plantations was another matter because no special enforcement agency existed. Thus, ordinary whites and slavers, became the "enforcement agency" who acted through brute force and violence, along with virulent racism.

A Few Slave Codes – Illegal to…	
Read or write	Marry legally
Own property	Own weapons
Stop separations	Inherit or bequeath property
Strike a white person	Beat drums or blow horns
Give evidence in court against a white person	
Leave the estate without a ticket or permission	
Practise Obeah (1760)	

The "ticket" system prevented captives from meeting others from different plantations but tickets were forged as enslaved literacy increased. British and Jamaican whites believed that educating captives was a complete waste of time, but captives educated themselves as some were literate. Although captives were forbidden to possess "horses, mares, mules, or asses", they did acquire them, but had no rights in the law to do so.

1735: An Act to prevent hawking and peddling, and disposing of goods clandestinely, decreed that: 'Mulattoes and Negroes were forbidden to sell any merchandise except foodstuffs', but later higglers were at the forefront of making and selling a wide range of foodstuffs as well as goods, handicrafts, and potteries etc.

1761: An Act to prevent … exorbitant grants and devises, made by white persons to negroes, forbade any "Mulatto or Negro" buying property; having any rights to land ownership or inheritances from whites because whites must prevent free Negroes but especially Mulattos from becoming equal to whites! This ensured former captives entered "freedom" with little to no wealth at all. Lack of land ownership is the main reason that the racial wealth gap exists today.

1788 and 1792: The New Consolidation Acts, were introduced as more captives died than were born. The truth is that these laws were enacted, to avoid constantly importing "New Negroes", and only to maintain or increase slavers' profits.

Divide and Rule: by Ethnicities, by Rewards, by Skin colour and by Clothing
- Slavers mixed their ideas of different African ethnicities together; *expecting support in the event of uprisings.*
- Skilled captives; drivers, sugar boilers etc., were rewarded with better living conditions; *to become informers.*
- Some "coloureds" were sent to England for their education or became servants escorting their owners about the Empire; *but if not recognised, worked alongside enslaved people.*
- Captives were given unbleached linen called 'osnaburg' from Scotland/Germany which *rotted away during field labour*; domestic enslaved were *given better clothing*. Steve O. Buckridge (2003) revealed that: 'Slaves' consumption of British textiles, contributed to the economic growth, longevity, and prosperity of the vibrant textile industry in Britain'.

Class system: white owners were at the top, but often lived in Britain; white professionals, traders or multiracial slavers, managed plantations. Next, were the multiracial or Black enslaved skilled labourers e.g., sugar boilers, blacksmiths, carpenters and so on. At the bottom of this hierarchy, were the Black sugar cane fieldworkers. Or the "common Negroes" and "head Negroes", as mentioned by Linton in his "confession" after a freedom movement (National Archives 1831).

The legacy of legalised cultural and racialised violence against Black peoples, sustained whiteness as the ideal to uphold. Most experts believe that this led to descendants experiencing intergenerational and multigenerational psychological traumas; known as Post Traumatic Slave Syndrome as identified and theorised by African-American, Dr Joy DeGruy Leary.

Chapter 7

GATHERING THE CANE.

Image 50: Gathering the Cane", Slavery Images: A Visual Record of the African Slave Trade and Slave Life in the Early African Diaspora

What was the spectacle of suffering?

'… permanent markings on [B]lack bodies in public places to terrorise others from committing the same crime', according Professor Pieter Spierenburg (1984). Such punishments became illegal under the **Jamaican Consolidation Act 1792**. It said:

> Any person or persons that shall wantonly or cruelly whip, maltreat, beat, bruise, wound, or shall imprison or keep in confinement, without sufficient support, any slave or slaves, shall be subject to be indicted.

Priscilla had both ears cut off for running away.… She was placed in chains, and sentenced to receive thirty-nine lashes on the first Monday in each month for a whole year. Quote 26: W. J. Gardner 1873 Sketches, Manners

But the truth is that this Act was not worth the paper it was written on. The Jamaican Assembly's only job, representing the British courts, was to maintain white supremacy and authority over Blackness. The "spectacles of sufferings", were highlighted in Professor Diane Paton's mid-eighteen century research in 2001:

Common Whipman was a hired flogger who carried out the legalised violence or slavers did it themselves. Property crime mostly used the whip. Floggings ranged from 39 lashes to over 300 and not always at once, for stealing animals such as sheep, goats, cattle, hogs, horses as well as sugar, coffee or other items of food. Consequently, floggings became normalised within white eyes.

Ordinary whites and slavers acted as "policemen" who became naturally "suspicious" of Black peoples. Not only was Blackness associated with "chattel slavery", Blackness also became associated with "criminality" in the minds of whites. Commonly, *'whenever you see a black face, you see a thief',* wrote Anon, Marly (1828). This was the prevailing attitude.

Mutilation included the loss of one or both ears and nailing the severed ear to public place; the splitting of nostrils, and or the cutting off a foot. Ordinary actions were criminalised, e.g. 'drumming, gathering or meeting together', as in the Slave Codes. Today, this legacy means that Black people are criminalised for normal everyday behaviour, deemed "suspicious" by whites. Which is known today as any activity carried out by Black people, termed "living whilst Black"!

Murder of a white person is treason and punishment resulted in being, 'hung up in body chains till he be dead', or 'staked down and made fast to the ground and burnt till he be dead'. Regardless of reasons or provocation, there was no defence in the law. But, if a Black enslaved was murdered by white slavers, there was no punishment nor recourse to legal redress. Jury trials were not allowed for captives or free Black people. The legacy of which means that, today Black people receive much harsher sentences than whites for minor or the same offences and their witness testimonies are given less merit.

Murder of another enslaved: 'to kill another enslave was to destroy valuable property'. So, captives were prosecuted but can be acquited if the murder of another enslaved was, in 'defence of his master's property'! Enslaved people can give evidence against each other and free Black peoples, but not against whites. Today whites call this "Black-on-Black" crime which is given much more prominence; is deemed to be more prevalent and more heinous than white crime.

'Transportation off the island became a favoured punishment', according to Robert W. Smith (1945) because 'the value of the slave could be recovered at the same time that a dangerous individual was removed from the community'.

The paradox is that, Black enslaved or free peoples were treated as chattel property but were criminalised, prosecuted and punished as people with "rights" that were defined by whites whilst having no real rights in the law of whites! UNESCO confirmed that: 'These notions are deeply embedded in the very fabric of many Western societies', (2021).

Yet the truth is that, the legacy of the British colonial system meant that the generations of Jamaicans have known nothing but violence, which became **'hidden in the ordinariness of everyday'**, according to Professor Gale L Kenny (2010).

Why were Black bodies disposable?

Image 51: Above: Carting Sugar, Rose Hill The Residence Of Edward Jackson Esq. A bridge over the St Ann's river - the home of Edward Jackson 1836. Below: ©Exterior of renovated Rose Hall today, near Montego Bay in St James Parish

By 1793, there were 710 rural plantations with 128,798 enslaved, claimed absentee slaver Bryan Edwards (1789). Although historian, Michael Craton (1997) puts the total to nearer 1,000 plantations. The truth is, initially dense lush forests had to be cleared to make way for crop plantations.

Historian Katherine Johnston (2020) has shown that "Black bodies", were chosen to be "exposed to dangerous environmental conditions", instead of white bodies! "Black bodies" were more disposable than white ones, so more and more were needed to cut down dense vegetation, clear tropical forests and construct roads despite the environmental hazards, in order to build:-

New Seville Plantation: this land was seized by the invaders and they built the first Spanish settlement, near where Cristóbal Colón first landed. It was the first to receive African captives; the 'first enslaved village' and the 'first extensive sugar works', according to JNHT (n.d.). The Great House was designed by Samuel Hemmings.

Mona Estate: up to 185 enslaved people produced sugar, rum and managed livestock between 1775 to 1839. Owned by UK Croydon brothers, William and Thomas Bond. Today the grounds contain the ruins of an aqueduct used to channel water for sugar processing. Now the location of the University of West Indies, Mona Campus which 'offers world class, accredited higher education programmes', (UWI).

Rose Hall Mansion and Plantation (Montego Bay): Rebecca Ann Palmer of "the white witch" legend; inherited the mansion on the death of her fourth husband. Legend said that she murdered all four husbands and haunts the mansion. She 'was found smothered between the mattresses with a horse whip in her hand', wrote slaver, John Broderick (1895) by captives, due to her cruelty.

Hibbert House (Kingston): Built in 1755 by Englishman Thomas Hibbert Senior where captives were held in basement cells before scramble sales. Robert Hibbert Junior (1769) owned Georgia Estate and Dundee Pen. He received 'compensation and reparations of over £10,530 for … 531 enslaved following abolition', (Legacies of British Slavery). Today, Hibbert House is the head office of the JNHT and said to be the "most beautiful house in Kingston".

In the building of these Great Houses and roads etc., through tropical rainforests, Black bodies were deemed to be "more disposable". Today, plantation Great Houses are either hotels or tourist attractions. E.g., Rose Hall Mansion was renovated by the current owners who hold "Duppy" (*Adópé* from the Ga language, meaning "ghost" or "spirit") night time tours.

What were the Pickney Gangs of Jamaica?

Worthy Park Estate (1640), owned by generations of the slaving Price family expanded to over 12,000 acres. They received £3579 3s 2d reparations in 1836 for 464 enslaved. Another amount of £5860 9s 11d was paid in 1838, as stated by the Legacies of British Slavery.

Today, the Estate has selective memory loss. It boasts about its million-pound annual turnover but none of which would have been possible without the 'heroic efforts of the Black slave population', (JJ, 1971) of centuries past.

Image 52: Gang labour of picaninnies learning how to harvest cane

The truth is, forced African labour, built miles of aqueducts that powered slavers' mills and factories; built miles of roads and bridges to and from shipping ports; built slavers' opulent Great Houses as well as their own cottages. Professor Jorge Giovannetti (2006) identified labour divisions on plantations as:

First Gang: 18-45 years who did the hardest back breaking work of digging and planting; and that they '... toiled as human beasts of burdens in the fields', claimed Richard Sheridan (1985). These were prime adult males who were "seasoned".

Females: some historians believed enslaved females did the back breaking work of digging and planting. Whites considered African females to be stronger for agricultural labour. Today, this has evolved into stereotypes of the "Strong Black Woman" (SBW); meaning that Black women must be naturally strong, resilient, self-contained, e.g., "superwomen". The truth is that the "SBW" both helps and hinders, but mostly resulting in mental-health stress related disorders.

Vagabond Gang: for the most disobedient enslaved; for habitual freedom seekers, so they can be more closely supervised to avoid further escapes. Those absent twelve months (changed to six months) were sold and transported off the island.

> *Sugar and water given to them [enslaved] when they become weary or the sun is too intensely hot.* Quote 27: William Beckford, a major slaver , 1788

Second Gang: adolescents from 12-18 years or pregnant women or infirm or elderly adults, not requiring heavy work or great strength; weeding, cleaning fields, factory floors, cane and trash. For adolescents, learning social and gender roles.

Third Gang: also called the Grass Gang were boys and girls after five or six years old, engage in light work such as feeding pigs, using a small hoe, weeding and gathering crops, banking soil and manure around the young canes. They also set traps for the thousands of rats who enjoyed feeding on young sugar cane plants.

Fourth Gang: 0-5 years called "pickaninnies", from the Spanish *pequenos ninos*, and were the "playful gang" that picked weeds and did other light work.

Fifth gang: mostly the elderly, disabled or over 50 years; laboured as watchmen, or drivers with large whips who supervised first, second and vagabond gangs; older women laboured as cooks, midwives and looking after "pickaninnies" in the third or fourth gangs. W. J. Gardner (1873), who was a missionary in Jamaica, observed that : 'During crop harvest time, captives worked all night'.

The truth is that the, **'plantation is a canker close to the heart of Black people'**, claimed the Jamaican Journal (1971).

What was gold versus life?

Experts believed that 12-13 per cent of Africans did not survive the Atlantic crossing and many died soon after landing. Leading to regular imports of "New Negroes". For those who survived, life was 'nasty, brutish, and short', claimed Jamaican Professor of History, Franklin W. Knight.

In the eastern part of Jamaica, livestock of cattle, mules, sheep, pigs and goats were bred because the soil was dry, sandy and stony. These were called Pens. Historians believed work in pens were more varied than on plantations. But slavers in both pens and plantations were brutal dictators. According to eminent historian Michael Craton: 'Many of the processes learnt in sugar mills were later applied to factories in Europe and North America Sugar mills'. Most plantations had in common:

- more absentee slavers than resident; living in luxurious and ostentatious or political style in Britain
- crushing mills caused injuries and mutilations. Many also, 'sweated in the odorous hell of the boiling houses', wrote Michael Craton and James Walvin (1970).
- "hot-houses" as hospitals; pickney areas; bell or watch towers; slavers' Great Houses; all built by captives
- enslaved cottages and villages and later, provision grounds

Image 53: Sugar mill at work. Below. Cane hoeing/holing 1849

- **"jobbing gangs"**, are gangs of young Africans who were hired out to other slavers so as to *not* overwork their own enslaved' or it was cheaper to hire "gangs" to dig holes for sugar cane planting; which was one of the most backbreaking tasks. Jobbing gangs have been compared to 'over-driven horses: . . . worked so much, that they do not last long. **'It is gold versus life'**, said Rev. Richard Bickell (1825).

Professor of history, Michael Craton (1978) said that, 'after four or five generations, . . .Those born into plantation life, knew no other home'. Thus, many were socialised, born and grew up in the institution of chattel enslavement. Inferiorities became embedded psychologically for some African people. However, the truth is that, Africans were not incapable or unintelligent. 'The records show that the enslaved population included engineers, builders, welders, wheelwrights - in short, practitioners of the most advanced skills in the then known world', according to the NLJ (n.d.).

The sugar factory was the most advanced technological process of the day and held by enslaved people, in trusted positions. White slavers, thought this would be repaid with loyalty, but a typical Jamaican phrase is to **"play fool fe catch wise"**. Which means, to pretend to be really stupid, and or child-like, to gain a victory over the powerful. Turning the tables on powerful enemies through cunning and trickery also came from the Ashanti Gold Coast trickster folk hero, in the form of part spider and part human, called Anancy. Today, Anancy trickster tales are told through children's stories.

Paradoxically, the "overgrown child-like" act fed into white stereotypes of Black people. Even though, slavers believed that the so called "cringingly docile" (Michael Craton 1978) captives, were loyal labourers, the truth is, that they were often the main instigators of freedom movements against the white supremacists need for **"gold versus life"**.

Who are the Higglers?

The irony of plantation gang labour and slave codes contrasted starkly with **Higglers**. The female Higgler or Huckster evolved, meaning 'a street vendor, a person who hustles to sells their wares', according to Prof. Smith (2006). Goods were "higgled" using pushy tactics at bustling markets.

The truth is that, most slavers focused on profits, and not feeding captives. To avoid starvation, captives were given **Negro Grounds** under the Jamaican Consolidation Act 1792, to grow "provisions" in their own "grounds".

The Act was aimed at increasing health, if fed properly; to avoid the expense of importing "New Negroes" as more died than were born. The "grounds" given contained poor quality soil, that were unable to produce sugar cane. Innovatively though, enslaved people repurposed their "Negro Grounds" and their "provisions" into unique spaces which was beyond the surveillance of slavers.

Now that "chattels" had their own "properties", the unique Jamaican "Higgler" evolved. They grew: 'Yams, cassava, pigeon pea, banana, okra, sweet potatoes, eddoes, callaloo, plantain, thyme, citrus fruits', said James Grainger (1764). Including fruits and vegetables, they also bred animals; animals that were brought over by the Columbian Exchange. Potteries and handicrafts were also made for sale.

Image 54: Above: Representation of the Exterior of a "Negro House", 1876 with ground provisions. Below: Going to market. Constant Spring Road (Schomburg Centre for Research in Black Culture).

By higglering, higglers set their own prices for their surpluses at various markets e.g., Shake-Hand Market, Portland parish, which were held on Sundays, the captives' free day. Higglers trekked with heavy loads or on donkeys, for miles and miles from the rural interiors to urban towns. White merchants often brought the produce of the enslaved for resale. Higglers thus, became the distributors and producers of a range of goods by the end of the 18th century.

James Hakewill (1825), observed that, 'nearly the whole of the markets of Jamaica are supplied with every species of vegetable and fruit by the over surplus of the [N]egro's produce'. W. J. Gardner (1873), a missionary, described the atmosphere of animals, yams, people and crafts, etc., as an "indescribable noise and merriment". It was a kind of "carnival". But Rev. Richard Bickell (1825) said that markets were the "bait of Satan"; interfering with Sunday worship.

Higglers were always on the move; passing information around on resistance movements and their oppressive existence, as shown by Sir Hilary Beckles (2019). **"Carry go bring come"** as the Jamaicans would say, meaning spreading gossip, and passing news of uprisings to each other. Sir Hilary Beckles (2019) explained that the 'hundreds of hucksters, not only blended in with those who may have been fugitives from the law but, they themselves, may have been fugitives as well'.

Traditionally, higglers were praised for their entrepreneurial spirits. However, as they are at the intersections of race, colour, class and gender, higglering became known as the occupation of lower-class poor Black women. Set in motion by whites who gave "Negro Grounds" to the enslaved only to reduce their expense of regularly importing "New Negroes". Today, thousands higgle in modern downtown Kingston's Coronation Market; opened by King George IV in 1939.

Who were the Wherry Negroes?

'To Mary West who now lives with me, a wherry and two [N]egro men called Thom and Orange', wrote Charles Knight in his 1706 will.

Charles Knight was a Kingston slaver of the Whitehall plantation in St Thomas' parish, (Legacies of British Slavery). Thus, African captives, were not only to be brought and sold, but bequeathed as well as inherited, as shown by Professor James Walvin (2013), until the law changed to prevent Black people, enslaved or free and multiracial people from acquiring property and land; an attempt to prevent Black people from becoming equal to whites!

Wherry Negroes were advertised by Thomas Craskell (Image 55). Thomas Craskell owned Green Vale Plantation in Manchester Parish and two Bushey Park estates. His six Jamaican born white children inherited over £2,800 approximately each, according to the Legacies of British Slavery.

Wherry Negroes ferried people and goods from the slaving ships to shore. Wherry Negroes, also worked as sailors in Kingston and Port Royal, but there was always the danger that they would be resold into enslavement.

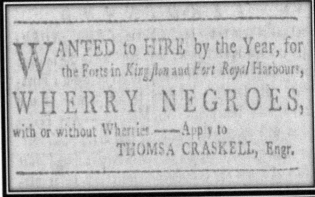

Image 55: Above: Wherry Negroes advert in the Jamaica Mercury and Kingston Weekly Advertiser: ©Michael Graham-Stewart Slavery Collection: 28 August 1779. Below: Black people in variety of jobs. Crew of HMS Linnet bartering for provisions in Cabinda, Circa 1853

Wherries were defined as 'the historical name for a slim, light boat, typically engaged in ferrying persons and goods across rivers'; easily stackable with origins in the historic Taíno Indians dug out canoes, according to William Sayers (2007).

Kingston's enslaved population grew from about 9,000 in 1774, 16,659 in 1788 to 17,940 in 1817 as Professor Trevor Burnard, Director of Wilberforce Institute, has shown. He wrote that: 'Many were re-exported in the 1780s and 1790s, to Cuba, Saint-Domingue [Haiti], Louisiana, Savanna, Providence, Cartagena, and Trinidad'. By this time, enslaved people in towns had multiple skills, although most mulattoes' shunned agricultural labour, preferring urban areas such as Kingston because, "agricultural labour was for Blacks" (Professor Burnard).

In towns, newspapers such as the *Jamaica Mercury* and *Kingston Weekly Advertiser*, advertised for "Butcher Blacks" and, "Blacks Acquainted with Driving of Cattle" (July 1779). Another advert said: "Wanted to Hire, two or three Light Negro Boys, to ride Post between Kingston and Monday Hill, who understand the care of Horses". "A Mulatto named James Crookes was, 'by trade a saddler', (1816 *Cornwall Chronicle*). Others also worked in 'ship carpentry, building and road construction, furniture making, coppering, smithing, tailoring', said eminent historian, Professor Barry W. Higman (2005).

Females mostly worked as domestics, cooks or seamstresses in urban areas, whilst rich white slavers returned to Britain with their fortunes; built beautiful country houses, provided libraries for Oxford colleges and art collections which now sit in UK's national galleries including the Tate galleries from sugar giants, Tate & Lyle, according to the experts.

Why was Jamaica, the jewel in Britain's Crown?

Before Jamaica became a Crown Colony between 1866-1944, it was one of the world's leading sugar-exporter, replacing piracy as the main source of British income. For example, Bristol imported 22,811 barrels of sugar in 1785, used to sweeten the newly fashionable British habit of drinking tea; as well providing "energy" for the mass of white British poverty-stricken labouring classes.

The truth is that, the 'British extracted the greatest per capita profits than any other European country and made the most money', wrote eminent Professor, Barbadian Sir Hilary Beckles (2007).

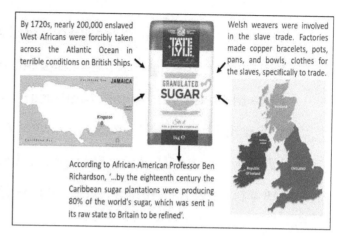

By 1720s, nearly 200,000 enslaved West Africans were forcibly taken across the Atlantic Ocean in terrible conditions on British Ships.

Welsh weavers were involved in the slave trade. Factories made copper bracelets, pots, pans, and bowls, clothes for the slaves, specifically to trade.

According to African-American Professor Ben Richardson, '...by the eighteenth century the Caribbean sugar plantations were producing 80% of the world's sugar, which was sent in its raw state to Britain to be refined'.

Historians confirmed that sugar production peaked around 1805 when Jamaica was the world's leading exporter, creating great wealth for Britain; exporting nearly 100,000 tons of sugar. At this point, **Jamaica's sugar was the Jewel in Britain's crown; the world's leading individual sugar producer.** The British peoples' sugar craze for cakes, biscuits, and confectionery was the White Gold until the 1846 Sugar Equalisation Act, ended the British monopoly on sugar.

Evidence has proven that the cheap produce and super profits of the plantation system accelerated the development of British seaport towns and the Industrial Revolution. For example, the Barclay family, owned slave plantations. From their profits, they set up Barclays Bank, which became one of the foremost trans-national banks in the 20th century until 1977. Then it was acquired by the National Commercial Bank of Jamaica; whilst Barclays became a major bank in Britain.

Coffee was the second most important Jamaican export crop. By 1832, there were 'approximately 45,000 enslaved people settled on coffee producing properties, in mountainous districts', (JIS n.d.) becoming the world leader in coffee exports. Today: 'Blue Mountain coffee, which is primarily exported to Japan, brings in some $12 million annually in foreign exchange earnings', according to the Food and Agriculture Organisation of the United Nations (FAO 2008).

Dr Hans Sloane (1688), an Irish botanist and doctor to the govenor, observed that: 'Bananas were grown freely on small acreages,' in Jamaica. Since the decline of sugar plantations, an American traveller reported that 'thousands of bunches of bananas are raised in Jamaica by the colored people, a few here and few there', (*New York Times* 1859). Higglers 'walked fifteen to twenty miles with ... bananas, coffee, chickens, in a basket on their heads', claimed African-American Professor Thomas Holt (1992). He said that: 'These were not a lazy people'. By 1866-1870, US whites capitalised on the freed peoples' banana initiatives. Jamaica then became the first commercial banana producer in the Western Hemisphere until the 1940s.

Henry Tate and Abram Lyle is said to have started the Tate & Lyle sugar company in 1921. They pride themselves on "not being alive" during the plantation era! However, the truth is that, Tate & Lyle's fortune was made by bringing sugarcane from Jamaica and other islands, refining some into sugar cubes in London and selling it on.

Henry Tate is called a philanthropist because his fortune led to the four Tate Art Galleries; the London Tate Gallery opened in 1897. However, the true source of the Tate's wealth lay in the African enslaved and emancipated people who toiled 7352 km away, out of sight and out of mind. Today, the Tates "Respectable Trade" is memorialised for their philanthropy with statues, libraries, factories, buildings and art in UK city centres!

Chapter 8

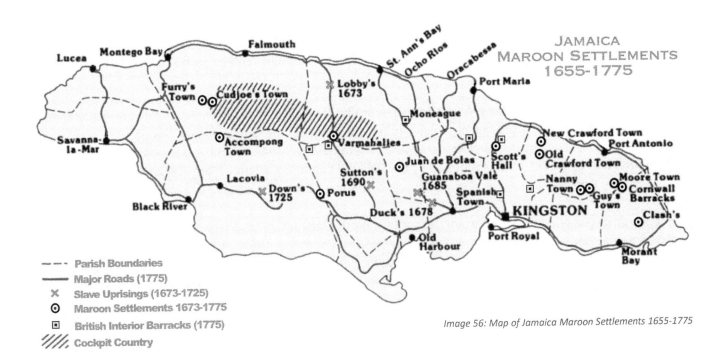

Image 56: Map of Jamaica Maroon Settlements 1655-1775

Who said "To manie negars and blackamoors"?

White Jamaican slavers travelled to England with their Black enslaved as servants. But, there were 'all ready her to manie', and a 'great number of negars and blackamoores', declared Queen Elizabeth in 1596 and 1601; 'ordering them out of the realme'.

Historians disagreed whether this was a deportation order for all "negars and Blackamoors" to be removed, or directed to, the ten Negroes exchanged as part of Spanish-Anglo negotiations, but instead, were left in England as prisoners of war when there were, 'all ready her to manie'.

Image 57: Third Duke of Richmond, hunting with his servant. Johann Zoffany, 1765

English Professor, Beth Fowkes Tobin (1999) wrote that when white slavers, 'established large communities in London, Bath, Bristol, they bought landed estates in the British countryside and 'commissioned … portraits that often featured their slaves'.

Whilst the Black enslaved in England were "fashionable signs of wealth and exoticism", they were in servitude. By the mid-eighteenth century, there were over **20,000 Black people living in Britain,** 'which are crept into the realme', 'of which kinde of people there are all ready her to manie'.

> *1596: Her Majestie understanding that there are of late divers blackmoores brought into this realme, of which kinde of people there are allready her to manie, … those kinde of people should be sent forth of the lande … to take those blackmoores that in this last voyage … to be transported by him out of the realme.*
> Quote 28: Queen Elizabeth Acts of Privy Council

The famous legal case of **James Somerset** or Sommersett ruled in 1772 that: 'No master ever was allowed here to take a slave by force to be sold abroad because he had deserted from his service', according to James Robertson (2008) of the University of Jamaica.

In 1771, James Somerset was baptised in Holborn, England. He escaped from his slaver, Charles Stewart's captivity but was recaptured, abducted and taken from England to Jamaica, shackled onboard the *Ann and Mary* ship. Lord Mansfield, a judge, together with abolitionist Granville Sharp (from the *Zong* Massacre), who defended Somerset, ultimately freed him on the grounds that slavery was so "odious" and, "that what was tolerated in the colonies was not accepted at home"!

> *1601: Whereas the Queen's Majesty is discontented at the great number of 'negars and blackamoores' which are crept into the realme … who are mostly infidels without understanding of Christ and his Gospel, in order to the discharge of them out of this country.*
> Quote 29: Cecil Papers: December 1601

Lord Mansfield declared that: **'I cannot say this case is allowed or approved by the law of England, and therefore the black must be discharged'.** Thus, setting a precedent for "negars and blackamoores", to sue for freedom in Britain (mostly England), and '… abruptly terminating the practice of black slaves ostentatiously escorting their masters about the empire', said Sandra Meditz from the Library of Congress.

Experts believed that the Somerset decision was spread to Jamaica, by missionaries, sailors etc., causing a, "culture of expectation of freedom", as Professor Julius S Scott (1986) puts it. So, some Jamaican enslaved people appeared to believe that they were "free" from this ruling, as Black peoples in England appeared to be but were not.

What were the hidden meanings of Jankunu?

"John Canoe", (English corruption), is the oldest Jamaican street procession, 'in keeping of "rites of rebellion", as eminent anthropologist, Professor Kenneth Bilby (2010) puts it; 'viewed as a necessary evil' and known as "negro balls" to whites. Eurocentric experts and some Black people believed Jankunu was "secular", lacking religious or spiritual meanings; only entertainment with some English "mummings", because enslavement obliterated homeland memories. The truth is, Jankunu combined:

African elements: rooted in honouring ancestors and initiation rites
- white masks or white powder is, 'a widespread practice in ... West Africa ... [and] among the Maroon peoples', said Professor Bilby (2010) which represented spirituality.
- Edward Long (1774) observed, 'robust fellows, dressed up in grotesque habits, and a pair of ox-horns on their head, sprouting from the top ... about the mouth ... with large boar-tusks'. However, horned cattle did not exist in Jamaica until the invasions.
- the gumbe drum in "spirit possession", is known as "myal". Survival of African religions (myalism and obeah) were hidden in these "fun" festivals, to 'safeguard African religious culture', said African-American Professor Dianne Stewart (2005), from whites.

Jamaican-African elements: costumes were meant to provoke awe and fear
- Koo-Koo, or Actor Boy, Princes, a Bull, a King or Queen participants with: 'Characters called Pitchy Patchy, the Devil, Belly Woman, Cow Head ... Indian [that] traversed the streets ...', wrote Dr Laura Smalligan (2011); this is the invention of enslaved culture.
- They 'carry short whips, which they crack loudly and dexterous', wrote a white Jamaican anthropologist, Edith Clarke (1927). '[T]he dancers tied rattles to their legs and cows' tails to their backsides and add[ed] such other odd things to their bodies ... as gives them a very extraordinary appearance', described Dr Hans Sloane in 1687 (1707).

Image 58: Above-Jankunu. Below- Queen of the Red Set Girls with whip in hard. Drawn by Isaac Mendes Belisario, a Jamaican Jew, in 'Sketches of Character' 1837

- white masks also mocked oppressors safely whilst identities were hidden. '[S]laves knowingly and ironically performing public put-ons of whites', (Prof. W.T. Lhamon 1998).
- the huge headdress of Jankunu may be a 'representation of a multi-storey West Indian house, complete with numerous red-framed windows', said Dr Smalligan. Subtly opposing the law which only allowed one window and one door in enslaved cottages, and or the headdress mocked slavers Great Houses and mansions.

English elements: costumes become more elaborate and less fearsome
- characters evoked excitement or fear in exchange for food and drink. Known as the custom of "mumming", (today's Halloween's trick and treating?)
- Red Set Girls represented the English and the Blue Set Girls represented the Scottish. Both tried to outdo each other in processions, dresses and entertainment.
- celebrating either John Conny or Eno Baise Kurentsi. Both successful African merchants along the Guinea Coast. But why captives would celebrate collaborators is not clear. Or Jankunu's roots lie in West Africa male secret societies, as some experts believe.

[H]e wore a most hideous head-dress ... pair of ox-horns, ... from the lower part of the mask large boar-tusks protruded .... Musicians, beating banjas and tomtoms, blowing cow-horns, shaking a hard round black seed, called Indian shot, in a calabash, and scraping the bones of animals together, which, added to the vociferations of the crowd, filled the air with the most discordant sounds. Quote 30: James Mursell Phillippo 1843

After emancipation Jankunu was seen as "pagan and immoral". Attempting to ban it, led to the Kingston Riots of 1840. However, the truth is that the Black peasantry subtly **'used culture as a means of rebellion through remembrance'**, wrote Professors Nicole Aljoe and Elizabeth Dillon (2017) although this aspect appears lost to the past.

How did fugitives remain fugitives?

Fugitives were **"hidden in plain sight"** as Professor Simon Newman (2018) has shown. "Hidden" amongst the dense populations of 'Black Jamaicans [who] made up eighty-nine percent of the island's total population of 280,000 in 1791', wrote slaver, Bryan Edwards (1796).

Hidden by, **"walking, running, and escaping"**, explained eminent Professor, Sir Hilary Beckles (2019), whilst "whites failed to see fugitives in plain sight". Professor Douglas Chambers' Documenting Runaway Slaves Project (2013) said that, 'advertisements personalise history, providing important clues about the lives of slaves'.

Hidden in plain sight: Accordingly, 'Advertisers could know to the very street, gate or yard where the [enslaved] were and still be unable to put their hands on them', (Professor Michael Mullin 1985). An advert for Coleraine said he will, 'endeavour to pass for a free man, and to get off the Island', in the *Kingston Journal*, (1789). Another advert in 1813 said, 'he was seen lurking about the Bogue Estate'.

A 1718 advert said, 'Calamante [Coromantee] Negro boy named Darby marked W.P. that used to conceal himself about the Town', (*The Weekly Courant*). In that year, another advert said: 'Negro woman named Venus, ... by intelligence she has hired herself in Kingston'. Another said that a: 'Runaway ... Apollo ... has been lately seen at east end of Kingston with fish', (19-16 June 1799).

New Negroes were often fugitives: the 1814 *Cornwall Chronicle* advert reported: 'James, a Coromantee, runaway since purchased as a new Negro'. Also, 'Quashie, a Coromantee, ... ranaway a new Negro and has no owner, no mark'.

Image 59: Above: ©Crossing The River On Horseback In The Night 1872. Below: An advert for Gloster in The Jamaica Mercury and Kingston Weekly Advertiser 1779

Others escaped brutality: Durham described as, 'a stout Negro man', who escaped after a two-day flogging in 1777. Listed in 1813 Morant Bay Workhouse was a Creole named Cudjoe, described as 'marks of cutlass chops on back'. St Andrew's Workhouse 1814 listed Bessy, as an escaped Eboe with 'marks of flogging'. In 1797, 'Hamilton fled with 'a chain and collar round his Neck' and ... harboured in Kingston', (*The Daily Advertiser*).

Separation: 'Dick was a good Negro till he got connected with Prudence', (1776) said one advert. Another said, "good-looking" and "14 years", two boys named London and Ben, were captured by a free mulatto in Spanish Town but saved by a higgler woman who claimed them as her sons. *The Jamaican Mercury* 1779, listed a mother and child, who had escaped, 'to where they have relations'. An advert for a: 'Creole Black Man named Trouble', who had 'relations about the Red Hills near Spanish Town, where it [he] is most probable concealed', (7-14 August 1779).

There were 7,428 known fugitive adverts in the 18th and 19th centuries

The truth is, despite severe retributions, many fugitives remained fugitives, who were "hidden in plain sight". These fugitives were the constant and relentless thorns in the British colonisation plans for Jamaica.

What did fight the Buckras mean?

Buckras meant white man in the Efik language. Eurocentric historians complain about the lack of "rebellions", but the truth is that, there were more than 400 revolts with major confrontations. Jamaican Professor and Sociologist, Orlando Patterson (1970), said there were 'numerous minor skirmishes, endless plots, individual acts of violence'. A few were:

Image 60: Jamaican slave revolt 1759. An imagined scene by artist: David, François-Anne (1741-1824)

1655-70: African enslaved fled during the Spanish-British battles. Leaders, Juan de Bolas agreed a British peace treaty in 1656 and in 1670 Juan de Serras was outlawed. Many fugitive seekers joined these new Maroons that were the sharpest thorns in the British colonisation plans.

1673: over 200 "Coromantees" on Major Sebly Lobby's estate in St Ann's, killed a dozen whites, plundered other estates and fled to the mountains. Later, they formed the Leeward Cockpit Maroons.

1675: freedom fighters escaped from a St Mary's plantation. Rewards were twenty pounds for Peter and Scanderberg, fifteen pounds for the Negro called Doctor.

1678: slaver's wife, Martha and other whites were murdered on Captain Ducke's plantation in St Catherine.

1685: 150 captives from St Catherine's Grey's Estate and Guanaboa Plantation, plus others from four nearby plantations seized firearms, totalling about 500 "Coromantees", killed eleven whites and lasted a year. Freedom seekers ran and hid in the mountains. Martial law was put in place to catch them, but with little success.

1690: 400 captives from Clarendon's Sutton Plantation, seized all arms; killed the white owner and burnt his house down. Survivors fled to the mountains. Led by a Maroon called Cudjoe.

1696: an uprising at the Paul Island Estate, Westmoreland, belonging to Julines Hering; his family were killed. Freedom seekers fled to the Leeward Maroons in the mountains.

1730-40: so-called first Maroon War. **1742:** Maroons stopped a "Coromantee" Christmas slave plot in St James's Parish.

1745: 'About 900 Negroes had form'd a plot to destroy all the white people, which was discover'd by a Negro wench....' (Anonymous (1745) *Letter from Jamaica from Gentleman's Magazine*).

1760: Tacky's Freedom Movement was a major civil unrest. **1765:** Blackwall's Revolt. Planters and their allies put down this revolt quickly. Punishment was severe. **1766:** Another so-named Coromantee uprising in Westmoreland Parish.

1770s: Three Fingered Jack, (Jack Manson) was "the famous [N]egro robber", said Benjamin Moseley (1799). A fugitive who killed his slaver and hundreds of white supremacists. The British saw him as a "Robin Hood" type. Living in the Blue Mountains, he "terrorised the whole island" for years; shot through the hand by Maroon Quashee earning him, his three-fingered name. Today, a heritage sign marks Jack's location near Eleven Miles village in St Thomas's parish.

1776: thousands rebelled in the parish of Hanover. **1784:** Grange hill plantation enslaved went on "strike"; "headed off into the woods"; resolved by sacking the cruel overseer. **1795-96:** the second Maroon war resulted in their exile.

1799: On December 23, French Jewish Isaac Sasportas was publicly "hanged by the neck until he be dead" (*The Royal Gazette* (Kingston) for conspiracy to free captives and start a revolution to extend France's power and empire in Jamaica.

Who were the Wild Negroes of the Look Behind District?

The Maroons, joined by hundreds of freedom seekers; living in the forested mountainous areas from the 1655-1660 Spanish-British conflict. Called "wild" Negroes, but "Maroon" from the Spanish word of "cimarron"; meaning "runaway cattle", "young pig", or "cattle gone wild", or just "wild". The truth is, Africans were far from "wild"!

It is a eurocentric myth that Africans accepted enslavement and Maroons were "wild savages". Historian Laurent Dubois, (2008) said that: '**The Jamaican Maroons, … were the most successful Maroon communities in the Greater Caribbean**'. Cromwell's soldiers were so fearful that a district was named **"Look Behind"**, because one soldier on a horse had to look ahead whilst another one had to look behind on the same horse in fear of Maroon guerrilla attacks. Even the world's biggest colonial military, could not defeat the Maroons in Jamaica!

Image 61: Leonard Parkinson, Maroon Leader, Jamaica, 1796. British Library

FIRST MAROON WAR 1655-1740: the resistance really started from 1655. The eurocentric myth exists that the First Maroon War started around 1728-1740. The truth is, that Leader Juan de Bolas, signed the **British First Peace Treaty in 1663**, against the Spanish, gaining land, freedom, and independence with privileges as "white British citizens".

The British troops still could not defeat the Maroons. By 1739, Cudjoe, born a Maroon, forced the British army to sign the **Second Peace Treaty.** This replaced the 1663 treaty. Land grants, freedom and self-rule in favour of the Maroons were some of the conditions. The truth is that the treaties were one-sided documents. In return, the Maroons had to act as "bounty hunters" with live-in British officers to ensure compliance but those officers were really spies.

Maroons 'held out against the forces of white men longer than any rebel troops', according to Professor H.A. Murdoch (2009) with an 'impressive display of guerrilla warfare', explained Professor Orlando Patterson. Slaver, Bryan Edwards (1798) said that Leonard Parkinson 'was the most obdurate and skilful of the young [M]aroon captains'. Quaco from the Windward maroons in the east, signed the **Third Peace Treaty in 1740,** though some believed it to be a traitorous sell-out. The truth is that five official Maroon towns achieved via treaties: Moore, Charles, Scott, Nanny and Trelawny, still exist.

SECOND MAROON WAR 1795: the Trelawny Town Maroons revolted against the British for months because the whites, 'flogged two Maroons convicted of stealing pigs', wrote NLJ (n.d.), meaning that the British broke their own treaties. But the truth is that the British were increasingly encroaching upon Maroon territory and where the hogs roamed. British martial law was proclaimed. Hunted and caught by bloodhound dogs, 500+ Trelawny Maroons surrendered or were tricked into exile to Nova Scotia, in 1796. Then exiled again to Sierra Leone by 1800.

Viewed as "traitors" because of their "bounty hunter" status, the truth is that, the Maroons also practised duplicity. But this is not mentioned enough in eurocentric accounts. For example, turning up late; taking their time to respond; providing false captures whilst aiding freedom seekers in the mountains, indicated a reluctance to fulfil treaty conditions. Today, the Maroons are proud of their victorious battles over the British, the world's biggest colonial military, symbolised by the treaties. Their audacious guerilla tactics and belief in freedom guaranteed their survival for subsequent generations.

The signing of the Peace Treaty is celebrated in Accompong Town every 6th of January. Since 2008, Moore Town, in the heart of the Blue Mountains, is safeguarded under UNESCO's Intangible Cultural Heritage of Humanity. However today, disputes regarding the exact nature of the treaty conditions, are being challenged by the current Jamaican government.

Why is Queen Nanny a National Hero?

Image 62: Above: Nanny's Grave, Moore Town in Portland.
Below: Nanny Statue in Ocho Rios Island Park

... old Hogg? [Hagg], who passed sentence of death upon this unfortunate man, had a girdle round her waste, with ... nine or ten different knives hanging in sheaths to it, many of which I have no doubt ... plunged in human flesh and blood; Quote 31: Lieutenant Governor, Phillip Thicknesse (1790)

The Jamaica Slave Act 1684 singled out the Maroons as "rebellious slaves". The Act also increased rewards for their captures. But the truth is that, The Right Excellent Queen Nanny (1686-c.1755) 'successfully evade[d] capture for years, even during the height of the British effort to exterminate her from 1730 to 1734', (Encyclopedia Britannica 2017).

"Nana", is an honorable title given to Ashanti chiefs, and **"ni"** means first mother, as SAGE Encyclopedia of African religion (2009) has shown; pronounced as **Nanny.** Queen Nanny, was the only female Maroon to be recognised as a freedom fighter and compared to fellow-Akan warrior, Nana Yaa Asantewaa who fought the British over the Golden Stool.

The truth is that, eurocentric historians believed Nanny to be mythical, because Maroon women were lowly "beasts of burden", as negrophobe Bryan Edwards said. Described as an "old Hagg", by 1790 Govenor Thicknesse, no one really knew what she looked like. Thus, an imagined image of Queen Nanny is presented as a national hero, on statues and Jamaica's largest banknote, the 500-dollar bill.

Stories such as, "hypnotising soldiers by staring into Nanny's boiling pot", compounded her mythical status, but the truth lies within some eurocentric distortions. The "boiling pot story" may have been the 900 feet drop waterfall, or the froth of the nearby rushing Stony River. SAGE (2009) said that, 'she was ... a powerful Obeah practitioner of folk magic and religion', and that she was, 'protected by a magical guard, consisting of a drink made of, *'rum, weed, and blood'*!

The mythical status of Nanny is disproven because evidence of a 500-acre Land Patent was registered on 20 April 1741. That land is called Moore Town after British colonial governor Sir Henry Moore. SAGE (2009) wrote that: 'Nanny vehemently opposed signing treaties with the British', but this patent in her name does exist, only mythical due to the eurocentrism and sexism of white supremacists.

Queen Nanny was a brilliant strategist using guerrilla warfare tactics in the Blue and John Crow Mountains. They raided plantations and welcomed freedom seekers. Over 800 enslaved were rescued, (SAGE 2009) and they fought off the world's largest army. They 'formed well-organised and efficient underground military units', according to UNESCO. Chambers Journal (1897) said the Maroons were 'a terror' and 'intimidated the whites from venturing to any ... distance from the sea-coast'.

Moore Town is now listed as Intangible Cultural Heritage of Humanity by UNESCO since 2008, to preserve the 'cultural heritage associated with the Maroon story. This includes settlements, trails, viewpoints, hiding places, etc., that form the Nanny Town Heritage Route'. Queen Nanny's legacy is the well-known **Jamaican strength of character, unyielding resistance and determination** in the face of adversity and oppression.

Chapter 9

Image 63: Roehampton Estate during the Baptist War By Adolphe Duperly

What was Tacky's Freedom Movement of 1760?

Taki or Tacky's Freedom Movement in 1760 was described by experts, as the greatest and most important enslaved freedom movement in the eighteenth-century British empire, sixty years before the Haitian Revolution.

Historians believed that Tacky was a military "Coromantee" Gold Coast leader. A significant point is that, regular imports of new captives meant that those born in Africa far outnumbered those who were born in Jamaica.

White slavers blamed insurrections on "Coromantees Chiefs" and disloyal Africans who were not the mass of docile enslaved, but savage, violent "New Coromantee Negroes", wanting to overthrow the white supremacists.

Tacky was kidnapped and enslaved on the Frontier Estate, owned by the Beckfords who were major white

Image 64: Enslaved rebellion, firing on the Negroes

slavers. Tacky and others are believed to have drunk a mixture of *gun powder, rum, blood and grave earth*, in oath-taking ceremonies, to invoke the warrior spirit in the realm of Ogun, as Professor Clinton Hutton in the *Gleaner Newspaper* (2015) has shown. African-American Professor Vincent Brown's research, found that the freedom movement consisted of three military planned uprisings rather than a "series of opportunistic riots" as described by eurocentric historians.

1) **St Mary's parish**: using their tactical skills to take weapons from Fort Haldane, the warriors went from plantation to plantation, destroying properties, releasing captives and killing white supremacists.
2) **Westmoreland parish**: a much bigger uprising took place, where the 'rebels selected a small and detached mountain range, … defensible from both planters and their maroon allies'.
3) **Clarendon parish**: survivors 'trekk[ed] through the foothills, into swamps, and to other detached peaks', where they attacked 'estates and then melt[ed] back into the wilderness'.

The rebels 'marched' to Whitehall, Haywood Hall and the Windmill. Bayly had quickly gathered a force of nearly 300, 'Whites and Blacks', and attacked the rebels, killing eight, 'the rest retreating into the wood. Quote 32: 'Zachary Bayley' (major slaver) Legacies of British Slavery.

The 18-month freedom movement left 60 whites dead, 500 Blacks dead or deported, another 500 executed and disrupted ideas of white settlement in the interior of a future Jamaica. The minority of whites were in a perpetual state of dread and fear. Damage was estimated at over a quarter of a million pounds. Tacky was eventually shot dead by a Maroon. His head displayed, on a pole in Spanish Town as the "spectacle of suffering".

The uprisings were reported in the UK. One headline read: "The Rebellion of the Negroes in Jamaica has for a long Time put a great Stop to Trade of all Kinds", (*Bath Chronicle* 1761). Meanwhile, the Seven Years' War (1756-1763), American War of Independence and the French Revolutionary wars (1792 and 1799) disrupted the sugar economy and British profits.

White revenge led to a new law called: *An Act to Remedy the Evils Arising from Irregular Assemblies of Slaves 1760*, which tried to outlaw Black people from meeting or gathering together for any reason. An expert once said that, "the circle of violence", meant Jamaica eventually became "one gigantic prison". But the truth is, torture, killings or rewards did not stop the majority of Black captives determined to "**fight the buckras**", and to "**tek force wid force**", for their freedom.

Why was Britain "ripe for abolition" by 1807?

Britain was ripe for abolition long before they passed the **Foreign Slave Trade Bill in 1806** and the **Abolition of the Slave Trade Act in 1807:** Historians disagree about the reasons.

Unprofitable? Tacky's 1760 Freedom Movement; Seven Years' War 1763 between Britain and France. The American Declaration 1776 'marked the beginning of the [British] decline', reducing American food supplies by 1780s. This meant: 'Fifteen thousand slaves died of famine in Jamaica', wrote Professor Williams (1977) or twenty thousand according to other historians. Britain's loss of thirteen American colonies in 1783; Britain at war with Napoleonic France 1803 to 1805 and that compensating slavers during a war, would be too expensive. Hence, abolition had nothing to do with "humanity" but unprofitability.

ANNO QUADRAGESIMO SEPTIMO

GEORGII III. REGIS.

C A P. XXXVI.
An Act for the Abolition of the Slave Trade.
[25th *March* 1807.]

Image 65: Slave Trade Act of 1807

> *Jamaican slaves were singing songs about the Haiti Revolution* David Geggus

Hugely profitable? The Jewel in Britain's Empire. Conversely, Professor Drescher has shown that the trade in Africans was deliberately destroyed by the Abolition Acts. After 1799, the profits oversupplied the sugar market according to Professor David Ryden, which 'directly influenced Parliament's final decision to abolish the slave trade'. He explained that the: 'Economic crisis faced by sugar planters was critical to the timing of abolition in 1807'. The continuous supply of new Africans at ever increasing prices produced too much sugar that, in turn, lowered prices of sugar, rum and molasses.

Humanity? relentless agitation, conspiracies, freedom seekers and movements from the Maroons, African-born and Jamaican-born people; Somerset decision of 1772; the Zong Massacre 1783; French Rights of Man 1789; and most importantly, the fear that the Haiti Revolution would spread to Jamaica. Whilst at the same time, abolition would prove that Britain was "enlightened, modern and superior" to rule a powerful empire.

Yet, Portugal abolished their enslaved trade in Madeira *before Britain in* 1775; the Danish gained 'international prestige', by abolishing their trade in human trafficking in 1792, *before Britain,* as Professor Pernille Røge (2014) has shown. France abolished their slave trade in 1794, again, *before Britain*! The truth is that, abolition became a "weapon of war" aimed at Britain's colonies', according to Professor David Geggus (2014), between the different war-ridden slaving nations.

The Abolition of the Slave Trade Act, 1807 stated that: 'all manner of dealing and reading in the purchase, sale, barter, or transfer of slaves or of persons intending to be sold, transferred, used, or dealt with as slaves, practiced or carried in, at, or from any part of the coast or countries of Africa shall be abolished, prohibited and declared to be unlawful'.

Yet the truth is that, the Act was not worth the paper that it was written on because Britain continued to profit in the trade whilst simultaneously, "clearing the competition from the seas". The **1807 Act** meant that the British Royal Navy attacked, searched ships and fined captains for each African "rescued", but this did not deter the slavers; it was still immensely profitable. Only the trade, was outlawed, not enslavement itself.

Once known as "Great Britain", Britain then became the "Great Abolitionist" of the 19th century. Changing their strategies with as much ease as the waving seas that they sailed on, because wherever there was profit and power, "Great Britain" will be there; singing their nation's song: 'Rule Britannia … Britons, never, never ever shall be slaves'!

What was the Ethiopian Baptist Freedom Movement of 1831?

'Jamaica was home to more rebellions than all of the other British islands combined', said African-American Professor, H.A. Murdoch (2009). Plantation owner, John Stewart (1823) said that, 'slaves who are Christians are generally more sober, steady, peaceable and obedient, than those who are not'. But he was completely wrong. The truth is, the largest, longest and most influential enslaved freedom movement was carried out by enslaved Christians called **Ethiopian Baptists.**

Founded in Trelawny Parish by African-American former enslaved, George Lisle, and Moses Baker, not white missionaries, the Ethiopian Baptists were popular, although slavers persecuted them. Historian, Mary Reckord (1968) noted that captives 'spiritual equality ... mingled ... with traditional African religious forms', [and] 'Black cultural consciousness'.

Samuel Sharp (Daddy 1780-1832), a former captive from the Cooper's Estate, not Craydon as stated on the Proclamation, was a passionate Baptist deacon, of the Thomas Burchell Church in Montego Bay. Able to read the Bible, he learnt that: "No man can serve two masters". He also preached from the British Parliament's abolition newspapers.

Image 66: Proclamation Government Reward for "rebel slave leaders"

Historians believed that captives protested because they thought they were already "free", but the slavers kept their freedom from them. Or, that the insurrection started because Christmas holidays were reduced from three to two days. Nonetheless, according to the *Kingston Gleaner* (1935), Samuel planned: "Jamaica's First Sit Down Strike"; which was meant to be peaceful and non-violent. If slavers refused to pay for their work on the extra day that they had lost, they would not return to labour, ruining the slavers' sugar harvests. As a precaution, others prepared for armed resistance.

Historians believed Gardener and Dove, calling themselves "The Black Regiment", first set ablaze the Kensington Estate. That fire 'carried the rebellion into the hills, invading estates and inviting recruits, burning properties on the border of St. James and setting off a trail of fires, through the Great River Valley in Westmoreland and St. Elizabeth', described Mary Reckord. Across the richest Jewel in Britain's Empire, fires lit up the skies with flames burning down plantations, buildings and crops. Historians believed either 18,000 or up to 60,000 enslaved were involved, (David Geggus 2014).

Slavers' revenge involved martial law; rewards for captures; destroying Baptist churches and blaming white missionaries as bad influences. Over 200 enslaved people were executed, a further 312 exiled or executed and 14 whites died with over £1 million in damages. Spectacle of sufferings included bodies left to rot, and heads stuck on poles in public places. These reactions were viewed as immoral, violent and "un-British" by whites in Parliamentary Westminster Britain.

Before Samuel was hanged in Montego Bay on 23 May 1832, he uttered: **'I would rather die upon yonder gallows than live in slavery'**. The UK's *Nottingham Review* reported that: 'Nothing will satisfy the people short of instant and complete extinction of the [N]egro slavery', (April 1832). That same month when Samuel was hanged, the British House of Commons appointed a committee to abolish slavery. This was the most influential result of great significance because, **within 18 months, the Slave Emancipation Act of 1833 was law.** Today, The Right Excellent Samuel Sharp appears on the fifty-dollar bill. He is a National Hero with statutes in Heroes Park, Kingston, and a burial site where he was hanged in Montego Bay.

When was enslavement really abolished, 1833 or 1834?

Neither. On 28 August 1833 the Slavery Abolition Act received William IV's royal approval, to take effect from 1st August 1834. This Act appeared to appease both the pro-slavers and white saviours. Furthermore, eurocentrics believed that white abolitionists ended slavery without any agency from captives, who were lost to the past. The truth is that:

Black people have always known about freedom and fought for an end to oppression. Thus, amelioration measures in the 1820s were eventually brought in, such as; reduced working hours; whipping females outlawed; religious instruction and enslaved marriages allowed, as Professor Wim Klooster (2014) has noted.

> *After 1st August 1834, all slaves in the British colonies shall be emancipated, and slavery shall be abolished throughout the British possessions abroad.* Quote 33: British Imperial Act 1833

However, not only were these improvements inconsistently applied, but a 'mass of evidence accumulated … that the slave system could not be improved, … only be abolished', argued English historian, Mary Reckord (1971) who lived in Jamaica. Thus, the 1815 Igbo Conspiracy took place when 250 Igbo men in St Elizabeth's Parish conspired to kill every white man in the land. More freedom movements followed in 1824, and 1825 as Professor David Geggus (2011) has identified.

> *… by nailing them down on the ground with crooked Sticks on every Limb, and then applying the Fire by degrees from the Feet and Hands, burning them gradually up to the Head, whereby their pains are extravagant.* Quote 34: Dr Hans Sloane (1701-25)

White Jamaican slavers were despised by white elite Britons for their excessively ostentatious displays of wealth; gluttonous habits and excessive, diabolical prejudice, cruelty and brutality. A magistrate and former slaver, John Stewart (1823), resident in Jamaica for twenty-one years, observed that, 'it [slavery] … may produce brutality of mind', and that, 'floggings were viewed with "savage gratification"; deterrents were 'most gross and open licentiousness continues … among all ranks of the whites'. Stewart concluded that, 'the most riotous debauchery prevailed on the estates'.

Compensation and reparations of £20 million enabled abolition. The British congratulated and glorified themselves. "We congratulate your Majesty on the final abolition of the African Slave Trade", as slavery was a, "stain on *their* British character", and "tarnished the honour of the British name". Nothing to do with humanity, only a "stain" to be involved.

Degrading: Once British whites decided that slavery was unprofitable, it then became a *stain on the British character*. With abolition as a weapon of war; Britain at war with every other nation; the British abolitionist propaganda of the passive, pitiful, and docile African enslaved, who needed saving from white greed by the British "white saviour complex" brigade, **£20 million reparations** was then paid by the British government to Jamaican whites, for the lost of their "properties". Hence, chattel enslavement was then said to have been abolished in 1834 but this was deceptive fallacy.

The truth is that, Black people were lost to history as eurocentric historians believed that only white British abolitionists were responsible for freeing captives. However, it was the freedom fighters and constant agitation by the Maroons, African captives, the Jamaican-born enslaved and then the Black emancipated, as one long revolutionary struggle. By the early 19th century, the **'constant threats and destruction on the plantations, was one of the chief reasons the British ended slavery throughout her Empire in 1833'**, concluded Dr James Lockett (1999). Additionally, the British feared that Jamaica would become another Haiti and that would be mortifying, considering it was a French colony!

Captives thought this Act was the freedom that they had been fighting for. Yet, the truth is, they were **not freed**. British slavery was replaced by an Apprenticeship scheme that was just **slavery in disguise**; to appease the pro-slavers; to further protect British profits, under the mythical delusional fallacy of teaching "freed people" about "civilisation"!

Why did apprenticeship replace enslavement in 1834?

Image 67: Emancipation 1st August 1834. James Phillippo.

1st August 1834 was a national holiday. Reports of that day, saw **Black people in holy joy, 'the chapel, the yard, and the streets around were crowded to excess' (JIS n.d.).** "We all free now! buckra can't catch we! hurra for fuss of Augus! hi, hi, fuss of Augus! hurra for fuss of Augus!", exclaimed one enslaved, reported by Irish magistrate, Robert R Madden (1835). But, "freedom" came in two stages. Apprenticeships in 1834 and then Emancipation in 1846, reduced to 1838.

Apprenticeships forced former enslaved to work for their slavers on the same plantations, without payment for up to twelve years so they could get used to "freedom"! Only children under six and those over 70 were immediately freed, because it was the "white man's burden", to ensure "chattels", were "civilised enough" for freedom. To compensate slavers for their "lost properties", would take another twelve years of free labour to pay for their own emancipation!

West India lobby were whites who fought to keep slavery going. Members of Parliament also delayed abolition for years because, enslaved people were "contented", anti-slavery was "absurd" and "impolitic"; all African people were "idle"; the work was not harder 'than that of our common labourers in England', said a *Pro-Slavery Letter* (1789). 'Suppose the [N]egro emancipated, what motive would he have for working?' exclaimed James Hakewill in 1825. Such sentiments were prolific. Hence, on the **1st August 1834**, apprenticeships replaced emancipation so whites could keep their power and money.

Apprenticeship, 'was only a modification of slavery, a substitution of half measures, … it was slavery disguised', wrote James Mursell Phillippo (1843), a white Baptist missionary in Jamaica for twenty years. He said that: '60,000 apprentices received … one-quarter of a million lashes, and 50,000 other punishments by the tread-wheel, the chain gang and other means of legalised torture'. Negotiating with former "chattels" as "apprentices" led to resentment by white slavers.

Richard R. Madden (1835), an Irish magistrate, wrote that: 'Since August various outrages have been committed by white people on [N]egroes', in his book called *"Twelve Month's Residence in the West Indies"*. He recounted an 18-year-old apprentice, James William from the Penshurst Estate who complained, that slavers were more "spiteful", than before slavery. 'I have heard my master say: "Those English devils say we to be free, but if we is to be free, he will pretty well weaken we, before six and four years done; we will be no use to ourselves afterwards".

Apprenticeship was a miserable failure and reduced to four years. "Freedom" came in 1838. Yet the truth is, the total worth of chattel property was £47 million with £20 million provided by the British government, only recently paid off in 2015. **The remaining £27 million was paid by the enslaved people during their period of Apprenticeship**, according to Eminent Barbadian historian, Professor Sir Hilary McD Beckles. True emancipation took place on **1 August 1838**.

What did "Full Free" mean in 1838?

'On that Emancipation day, many slaves were said to have walked up hills and climbed trees so as to clearly witness the literal dawning of their freedom', known as **"Full Free"**.

Image 68: Scene on a West Indian Plantation: The Enslaved Receiving the News of Their Emancipation

On 1st August, 1838 in Jamaica, '800,000 African bondsmen were made fully and unconditionally free', wrote John Stewart, a 19th century magistrate and former slaver, or 323,000 according to other historians. Today, every August 1 is Emancipation Day, a national holiday and celebration of the abolition of enslavement. A hearse containing shackles and chains that had been used to shackle rebellious slaves, was driven through the streets of the capital Spanish Town, and ceremoniously burned, according to *The Old Gleaner* (2001).

Unsurprisingly, freed people left their plantations in droves, now known as the **"Black peasantry"**. But vagrancy laws, did not stop the "flight from the estates", as Professor Christopher Bischof (2016) puts it. Immigration was the alternative to, 'counteract the emancipated demanding high wages', said Professor A. Murphy (2016), on contracts of up to seven years. Called indentured labour, immigration was meant to replace the Black peasantry's "flight from the estates":

1834-1838: 1,210 German immigrants arrived and settled in Seaford Town, Westmoreland parish
1835-1841: more Irish and Scottish arrived; Africans from Sierra Leone and from other Caribbean islands
1845-1917: about 37,000 Indians (mainly Hindu) arrived on indentured contracts; outlawed in the 1920s
1854-1900s: about 6000 Chinese arrived from China, Panama and British Guiana

Indenture saw a **new kind of slavery**. Derogatively called "coolies", Indians were, 'cheated, starved, flogged, and murdered', and that 'these wretched, hungry, houseless and outcast spectres [skeletons] picking up in the street a chance bone, [and] putrid offal', said the Governor of Jamaica, Edward Eyre in 1862.

The "flight from the estates", meant 140 sugar and 465 coffee plantations disappeared into the wilderness by 1860. To reverse this decline, UK Liverpool brothers William and David Smith, built the first steam railway in 1845, only 18 years after Britain, to transport crops quickly to the coast. Built by '500 freed Negroes', who 'never found any of them deficient in their capacities as workmen, or lazy and indolent', reported the *Freedman Anti-Slavery Reporter* (1866). Today only bauxite and sugar cane is transported, although passenger services are planned in the future.

I rejoice I am a slave no more, and you are slave no more, Jamaica is slave no more. Amen!"
Ex-slave, Thomas Gardner, NLJ

Land disputes arose constantly. Cottages were demolished or freed people were evicted as "squatters". As well as "Free" villages, land settlement schemes started as slavers refused to sell land to Black people or raised prices so high, that they could not afford it. *Try See Village* in Runaway Bay, St Ann's parish was one land resettlement scheme. The people could *"try"* and *"see"* what could be done with the land to start a new life. Furthermore, many "Full Free" people "gaan a farin" (gone to a foreign country), to Panama to build the trans-isthmian railways or laboured in Cuba, just 144 km away.

The truth is that, between 1850-51, 2000-3000 people died in cholera epidemics. New taxes on land, food, etc., meant to force former enslaved back onto the plantations, culminated in the Toll Gate uprisings in 1859. One former enslaved remarked; **"What kind of free this? This free worse than slave, ... This the free them gee we?"**, (Lorna Simmonds 1984).

How significant was the 1865 Morant Bay Freedom Movement?

'Enslaved people launched more revolts in Jamaica than in all other British colonies', said historian Devin Leigh (2020). The struggle against white supremacy continued under racist laws and structural inequality, despite emancipation and "freedom".

Image 69: Location of Morant Bay Freedom Movement

By 1865, '**a rebellion of wide proportions burst forth, like a destructive volcano**', said white Baptist missionary, Edward Underhill. A series of Underhill meetings with the Ethiopian Black Baptist communities, took place. Although Governor Edward Eyre had identified that: 'Deterioration, decadence and decay were everywhere noticeable', reforms were ignored and blamed on Black peoples' "laziness". High taxes collected from the Black peasantry only benefitted whites, who maintained a system as close to enslavement as possible. Biracial magistrate, **George William Gordon** (now a National Hero) said Governor Eyre "was a plague spot on poor Jamaica".

Paul Bogle, a Black Baptist leader, preached about injustices. Paul was a supporter of **George William Gordon**, who advocated for the rights of the Black people in the House of Assembly. Paul Bogle lived in the Free Village of Stony Gut in Morant Bay. One land dispute resulted in the prosecution of a villager for trespassing to recover his horse. Angry crowds protested outside the Morant Bay courthouse. The Riot Act was read. The crowd refused to disperse and were fired on. They retaliated by killing the chief magistrate and other whites. Arrest warrants were then issued for Paul and others.

Paul Bogle marched with hundreds of followers, into Morant Bay that, 'burst forth like a destructive volcano'; beating drums, blowing cow horns (abengs), carrying fishing spears, cutlasses, machetes, firearms, onto symbols of "white oppression", as Professor Gad Heuman (1994) has described. Thus, the issues of land ownership and justice had collided. These protestors 'took control of the parish and put the white plantocratic ruling class to flight'.

However, 'for an extraordinary period of thirty days', explained Professor Howard Fulweiler (2000), Governor Eyre implemented a savage misuse of martial law; known as the "**Killing Times**", by Professor Gad Heuman (1994). The protestors did not resist but over 400 other people were shot on sight; 600 were flogged and thousands of homes were burned by the British Troops and the Maroons, (as bounty hunters), under Colonel Fyfe, the British Captain. A reward of £2,000 for Paul Bogle's capture was proclaimed. Both accused of treason, Paul and George were hanged in October 1865.

A Royal Commission in 1866 found that martial law "punishments were excessive, barbarous, and "un-British". Hence, the Jamaican plantocracy government, the Jamaican Assembly, dismissed itself, making way for the **Crown Colony government which meant direct rule from London's Westminster Parliament.**

Paul Bogle's freedom movement achieved a significant change in Jamaica, that petitions and reforms could not. Experts believed that the 1865 freedom fighters became the foundation of the modern Rastafaris and the Jamaican working-class movements. Today, both Paul and George are National Heroes with statues in Kingston's National Heroes Park.

The truth is, not only did direct British rule reinforce institutionalised racism, but the British viewed themselves as victims of "selfish ungrateful Negroes". Those Negroes should be loyal to the British for giving them their "freedom", and not riot!

Chapter 10

Image 70: *View of Harbour Street and King Street, Kingston by James Hakewill, A Picturesque Tour of the Island of Jamaica, from Drawings Made in the Years 1820 and 1821. Note the design of the waving flag.*

Who were the Sons of Africa?

African freedom fighters who toured and campaigned for abolition around the UK. These Sons of Africa were prominent spokesmen for London's Black community and enslaved peoples but have only recently been recognised for their influences, abilities and efforts.

The Sons of Africa contradicted the white racist "ignoble savage"; "grateful slave" stereotypes; the "Ham curses"; "scientific racism" and so on, that saturated white society.

Ignatius Sancho (1729-1780) was a prolific and sophisticated writer who also composed music. He was regarded as "the extraordinary or exotic Negro stereotype". Thomas Clarkson (1786), a prominent British white abolitionist, argued that Ignatius Sancho, provided proof of "African genius"! Historians believed Ignatius was born enslaved during the "middle passage", although Ignatius referred to himself as a "poor African". He was either enslaved in Columbia or Grenada.

Image 71: Above: Ignatius Sancho, 1768 by Thomas Gainsborough: By Gilbert Stuart - National Gallery of Canada.

Ignatius Sancho wrote that: 'I am not sorry I was born in Afric[a]', (1784) in his letters which contradicted Thomas Clarkson's statements. Ignatius was a butler to the powerful Duke of Montagu family in Greenwich, London, UK where he was educated. He became an outspoken opponent of chattel slavery. In 1733, upon retirement, he bought a shop in Westminster, central London.

... the horrid cruelty and treachery of the petty Kings ... encouraged by their Christian customers ... who carry them strong liquors ... to enflame their national madness – and powder – and bad fire-arms – to furnish them with the hellish means of killing and kidnapping'. Quote 35: Letters of the late Ignatius Sancho, 1784

Ottobah Cugoano (1757- ?) also known as John Stuart, was the 'Noble or Royal African stereotype' because he was 'blood relative to a Chief before abduction'. Born on the Gold Coast of Fante heritage, he was kidnapped and taken into slavery. He wrote that he was 'delivered from Grenada and that horrid brutal slavery', to England.

Ottobah Cugoano was purchased as a servant to a Richard Cosway, he became literate and 'sought all the intelligence I could'. To further his abolition cause, he wrote appealing for Christian indignation at the British slave trade and enslavement; counteracting their excuses and justification from whites, with great clarity and insight.

... many even now are suffering in all the extreme bitterness of grief and woe, that no language can describe. The cries of some and the sight of their misery, ... but the deep sounding groans of thousands, ... great sadness of their misery and woe, under the heavy load of oppression upon them, Quote 36: Thoughts and Sentiments Ottobah Cugoano 1787

Ottobah Cugoano wrote an influential book in 1787, detailing his enslavement experiences. Together with **Ignatius Sancho** and the well-known **Olaudah Equiano**, these **Sons of Africa**, overcame some of the racist and pro-slavery doctrine of slavers, merchants and traders, monarchs and financiers etc, in Bristol, Liverpool, London and Glasgow, using reasoned arguments that appealed to the British "Christian" nation.

Historians believed that Ottobah was the first African who called for the worldwide slave trade abolition; emancipation of Caribbean enslaved and punishments for slave owners in 1787. Even more radical because he was a former captive, living in "Christian" Britain that had grown wealthy through the enslaved labour that he was campaigning against! Professor of English, Mukhtar Ali Isani (1997) termed this as, 'the irony of Christians tolerating slavery'.

Who were the Jamaican Jews?

Since 1834, The *Kingston Daily Gleaner* newspaper, started by Jewish brothers Jacob and Joshua DeCordova, is still owned by their descendants. Formed at the end of British enslavement, and known today as *The Gleaner*, it is a huge multimedia company, that has covered, 'every significant event in the history of Jamaica', (Jamaicans.com).

Some Jamaican Jews showed compassion towards enslaved people, the emancipated, the freed and also criticised the government. Fleeing the Spanish Inquisition, their numbers have remained small but disproportionate to their influence. Neither white nor Black, they were more white than Black because **Black people had the permanent stamp of enslavement on their skin.**

Image 72: Above Colonel Fyfe with the Maroons. How many Maroons can you see? There are more than you think!

Jamaican Jews, had "**white privileges**". They were members of the Assembly, had the vote as land owners and influence in newspapers. E.g., Sidney Lindo Levien's *The County Union* newspaper (1840s) who was prosecuted for his criticism of Governor Eyre's Morant Bay "Killing Times", but was later freed. Jamaican Jews worked as 'traders, merchants, planters, pen keepers (farmers), physicians, fishermen...', (Professor Stanley Mirvis 2020) as opposed to life in chattel enslavement.

One trader was Jewish Isaac Sasportas; 'of considerable means' and 'travelled from island to island in the Caribbean trading in textiles', wrote historian Zvi Loker (1981). In 1799, French officials conspired with Isaac and others, to invade Jamaica under French imperialism, but that plan was discovered. Eurocentrics believed that Isaac was a French patriot or radical idealist. Hanged in Kingston, Jamaican officials wrote "spy" on his chest before his execution (Zvi Loker 1981).

Nonetheless, most Jamaican Jews lived in urban areas. E.g., Jew Street in Port Royal before the earthquake; Jewish Quarter in Kingston before **"white flight"** to Uptown Kingston. The truth is that: 'Jewish slave owners in Jamaica are indistinguishable from their non-Jewish neighbours', concluded Professor Mirvis (2020).

Transcription: Kingston Gleaner report of The Morant Bay Rebellion, 19 October 1865, entitled "The Maroons". This wonderful and loyal people [the aboriginees of Jamaica,] have, under Col. A. G. Fyfe who led them in the last rebellion, turned out for the government to clear the mountains of St. Thomas in the East of the rebels who seek shelter in the natural wildness of their strong holds.

Their appearance, decorated with their well-known "war paint;" covered with bushes and twigs of the Lignumvitae, struck terror into the hearts of the rebels at Portland and St Thomas in the East. When they lay down nothing was discernable of their bodies, -nothing but the living bush that covered them. In this way they march without observation, and in this way they spring like tigers upon their prey, who, seeing nothing but a forest of bush, imagine themselves secure.

They are already scouring the countryside for the rebels, dragging them from their concealment, and exterminating them wherever they have been found. Over one hundred rebels are reported to have been shot by the Maroons in this mission already. At the execution of the rebels, and while the dead bodies were hanging as a public example, the Maroons (we are informed by Col. Hunt) assembled around the gallows, where they had a war dance; the savage wildness of which was truly grand.

The last line reported how successful Governor Eyre and the slavers were in turning public opinion against the freedom fighters. Before Govenor Eyre (Jamaican Assembly) was dismissed, they paraded the Maroons as "saviours" of the island! But equally, many of the Black peasantry and multiracial people supported the freedom fighters.

Who was Mary Seacole, Nurse or Imposter?

A Jamaican woman, born in 1805, who wrote her autobiography in 1857, entitled *The Wonderful Adventures of Mrs Seacole in Many Lands*. Mary's mother, a free African and doctress, ran Blundell Hall boarding-house in Kingston; which now houses the National Library of Jamaica (NLJ n.d.). Her mother was a doctress and where Mary learnt her skills in the 'prognosis and treatment of tropical diseases, general ailments and wounds', wrote medical historian, Dr Mariella Scerri (2020). A Scottish soldier in Kingston's British Army, was Mary's father.

Image 73: Mary Seacole's grave in London, UK

Mary's mother and husband died, and Blundell Hall had burnt down, but that did not stop Mary's dreams. Refusal by Florence Nightingale to nurse the war wounded in the Crimean War, did not stop Mary either. Determined, she opened the British Hotel near Spring Hill at Kadikoi (Turkey) for wounded war soldiers. 'Her work ... during cholera and yellow fever epidemics, had earned her a reputation as a nurse, and the title of "yellow doctress", said Professor E. Hawthorne (2000). However, Mary was lost to history but revived as an imposter to eurocentrics because:

Mary had not worked in hospitals: but the truth is that eurocentrics forget the structural racism that excluded Black people from "white" jobs. William Russell, the renowned Times correspondent in the Crimea in 1854, who witnessed and reported evidence of Mary Seacole's skills wrote that: 'I have seen her go down under fire ' as well as, 'a more skilful hand [for] a broken limb could not be found among our best surgeons'.

Mary was not a nurse: but no formal "nursing qualifications", existed in Mary's time, and herbalists skills were rejected. Although, '[t]he use of traditional medicine ... in the ... plethora of diseases is pre-historic and dates back into antiquity', wrote Razak Gyasi (2015). In 1703, Dutch merchant Willem Bosman said: 'The green Herbs ... amongst the Negroes, are of such wonderful Efficacy, that tis much to be deplored that no European Physicians has yet applied himself'.

Mary was a "sutler": meaning a lower-class person 'who follows an army ... to sell provisions', said Amy Robinson (1974). The British War Office, Medical Office and Crimean Fund turned her down to nurse and assist in the Crimean War. So Mary ran businesses to earn money, whilst nursing the troops, whereas white nurses only had to focus on nursing.

Mary was not Black: but she wrote: "I have a few shades of deeper brown upon my skin, which shows me related, and I am proud of the relationship, to those poor mortals whom you once held enslaved". Soldiers described Mary as Mother (symbolism for British) to her soldiers (British sons). Britain was promoted as the "mother country" correcting and civilising the "infant children" in her colony of Jamaica. Mary played into those notions because every aspect of society, was saturated with negative racial stereotypes.

Mary valued "whiteness", over "Jamaicanness"; i.e. an identity crisis, solely because: 'Her narrative is not one of victimisation, endurance, survival, but of accomplishment and achievement', said Professor Sandra Paquet (2017), a Caribbean expert. The truth is that Mary combined a travel book, as an autobiography cleverly: 'Minimis[ing] her ancestry and maximis[ing] ... knowledge and practice', said Professor Paquet (1992), to sell her book. Returning from the Crimea nearly bankrupt, Mary Seacole made enough money from the profits of her book, to live well. She died wealthy.

'*Wonderful Adventures* is a celebration of the brains, wit, charm, talent and energy of its self-proclaimed heroine, Mary Seacole', concluded Lorraine Mercer (2005), a literary theorist. Mary was a nurse, an entrepeneur, an author and a globe-trotting traveller. Buried in St. Mary's Cemetery, UK, a large statute was erected in 2016 in the grounds of London's famous hospital, St Thomas. Erected in her honour in the face of structural and overt racism, and in recognition of her skills.

What were the mad messiah myths of Alexander Bedward?

Alexander Bedward, said to be a "Prophet" and the "Black Christ", dared to remind his 30,000 followers, about the "Morant Bay" War; dared to call out the Governor and colonialists as "hypocrites, robbers and thieves. They ... are all liars .... Hell will be your ... portion if you do not rise up and crush the white men", (*Kingston Daily Gleaner,* 1895). Bedward also said: 'Whites were the Anti-Christ ... sent to plague the true people', reported *The Gleaner* (2021).

Image 74: Bedward Church in August Town, St Andrew's Parish. Now in ruins. Named August Town after the month of Emancipation in 1838. Jamaica Cir 1905, Collection Historic Jamaica

Bedward was the founder of Bedwardism. Subjected to continued British white supremacy, many Jamaicans turned to religion for salvation. As the Black peasantry became literate, they identified with the Biblical Ethiopians. 'Slavery, in the view of Ethiopianists, is a cardinal sin, exacerbated by the whites hypocritically calling themselves civilised Christians', wrote African-American Professor Charles Price (2003).

Bedward was born poor in August Town, St Andrew's parish in 1848, and suffered from mysterious diseases. Low wages on the Mona Estate led him to work and seek remedies in Panama, where he had remarkable and disturbing visions. By 1885, he returned to August Town and begun preaching from the Baptist Free Church, on the Hope River, in 1891.

Bedwardism believed Biblical Hebrews were their direct ancestors and Africa was their freedom from white oppressors. They wore white robes and believed in fasting and praying. *"Oh! dip dem Bedward, dip dem, dip dem, in di healing stream",* sung his followers whilst baptising them from their spiritual or physical afflictions, in the Hope River. '[P]ilgrims carried jugs of [Hope River] water to every part of Jamaica', said, J.M. Washington (1980) believing it to cure ailments.

Bedward was sent to the "Lunatic Asylum" in 1892 and 1895. Once for his "visions", and once for his "Black Nationalist" messages that were regarded as sedition. Meaning inciting others to rise up against: "Our Lady the Queen Her Crown and Dignity". However, Jamaican Professor Carolyn Cooper (2015) is adamant that: 'We must emancipate Bedward from the lie of lunacy'. Further "mad messiah myths" spread by British colonists and believed by some Black people were:

1. 1920: "Flying to heaven from an ackee or breadfruit tree", and then ridiculed as "the flying preacher man". But another Jamaican, Marcus Garvey (b.1887), became prominent. Hence, Bedward retired figuratively as in the Biblical Elijah who, "ascend[ed] into Heaven in a flaming chariot". People took this to mean he could "fly".
2. 1921: "Overthrowing the government". A "Manifestation" meeting in Kingston Park where he would "manifest" to his followers, that his time was up. Bedward knew that he would be arrested and "sacrificed" as in the Biblical Jesus.

Bedward was not a lunatic but a brave faith healer who sought to uplift the Jamaican people, but he also had some flaws e.g., "ascending into heaven". However, the truth is that, he 'was a charismatic leader; a beacon of hope for many disillusioned, impoverished, landless and jobless people, who were still suffering from the negative psychological and mental impact of slavery', reported *The Jamaica Gleaner* (Paul Williams 2015). He died in 1930 in the "Lunatic Asylum".

Bedward took on the British colonial forces, created an alternative perspective other than Blackness as inferior and uncivilised as shown by Dr David Gosse (UWI 2021). The legacies of Bedwardites evolved into Garveyite and then Rastafari movements who were also persecuted and harassed. Colonial white authorities decided that Black people asserting for equality were "epidemics of insanity", and locked individuals up in "Lunatic Asylums", or jailed for vagrancy and sedition.

Why is the Right Excellent Marcus Mosiah Garvey a national hero?

His remarkable life, as a man and movement. Born in St Ann's Bay in 1887, of Maroon heritage, he gave, 'hope for the oppressed masses by inciting "racial mobilisation", according to Professor Simboonath Singh (2004). He died in 1940s London but is buried in Jamaica's National Heroes Park. Garvey is credited with these phrases (JIS n.d.):

"Africa for the Africans, at home and abroad"
"Black is beautiful"
"One God! One Aim! One Destiny!"

Image 75: Marcus Garvey as commander in chief of the Universal African Legion, also set up Black Cross Nurses. He believed economic success was the quickest and most effective way to independence.

Some organisations and businesses he founded were:

1. **UNIA:** Universal Negro Improvement Association to dispel lies about the African's inferiority via education, and to trade with Africa for economic independence. Garvey set up New York Headquarters in 1906, addressing crowds of up to 25,000 and had offices worldwide. Professor Singh (2004) said it was: 'One of the largest Pan-African movements in history'.

2. **Newspapers:** *The Negro World, Blackman, Voice of the Negro* where he advertised his UNIA plans. Quotes from his speeches became iconic, e.g., *"A people without the knowledge of their past history, origin and culture is like a tree without roots"*. But, both the British and the US eventually banned what they called the "evil influences" of his newspapers.

3. **African Orthodox Church:** 'Erase the white gods from your hearts', urged Reverend George McGuire, a follower of Garvey's philosophies. 'Christianity is nothing more than an arm of white racism', said Professor Watson (1858) who described the Jamaican poor, as 'masses for whom hunger, poverty, illiteracy, and simple human misery are a permanent feature of their lives'. This church taught Psalm 68, which said: *"Princes shall come out of Egypt; Ethiopia shall soon stretch out her hands unto God"*, for redemption from their human misery. However, whites and some Black Leaders believed he was "foolish", a "buffoon", a "clown", and was ridiculed but decades later, this psalm seemed to have come true.

4. **Black Star Liner:** a fleet of ships for "Back-to-Africa" trade and repatriation for skilled persons. More than four million members invested. Prof. Ramla Bandele (2010) said that, 'given the racism and constant battles with white racists … many were reconsidering emigration to Africa'. The Black Star was eventually adopted by modern Ghana's national flag.

The **Black Star Liner** failed due to, economic downturn, shipping complexities and government interference, according to the experts. Professor Bandele (2010) said that the British, 'did not want gold production disrupted in the Gold Coast'. The US believed that, 'it was a British masquerading plot to re-control Caribbean and South American markets'. Therefore, Garvey was falsely jailed on mail fraud in the US. But, in 1988 the US said that those charges were, 'not substantiated and his conviction … was unjust and unwarranted', according to Professor Rupert Lewis (UWI 1997).

Eurocentrics believed that Garvey's repatriation schemes were utopian; that he was incompetent, and ill-informed about white peoples' racism. However, his achievements in the face of outright hostility, structural racism and overt prejudices are to be celebrated. The truth is that, 'no one could have organised and built up the largest Black mass movement in [African]-American history, in the face of continuous onslaughts … and the most powerful governments in the world, and yet be a buffoon or a clown', concluded Professor Adam Ewing (2011). Since 1992, the Headquarters of UNIA, Liberty Hall, is now a Kingston museum of Marcus Garvey's life and works, (JNHT).

Chapter 11

Image 76: Sound Systems in Jamaica © VisitJamaica 2018

Why do Rastafaris believe in Haile Selassie?

Jamaica is the birthplace of a worldwide movement known as Rastafari. 'More than 100,000 Jamaicans identify Rastafari as their primary religion, while many more Jamaicans accept the ideas of Rasta', according to the SAGE Encyclopedia of Global Religion (2012); the only new religion to have evolved in the 20th century.

Image 77: Rastaman on Negril beach

Rastafaris 'roots may be traced to 19th century slave revolts such as the Morant Bay Rebellion of 1865', wrote SAGE (2012). But emancipation in 1838 was not the end of captivity because injustices, poverty, structural and institutionalised racism were rampant and saturated society.

1963 Coral Gardens Massacre (former Maroon cockpit country) took place when the British gave "license to kill" Rastas and declared, "Bring Rastas in Dead or Alive". Dreadlocks were cut; camps evicted; arrests made and some killed. The truth is that, officials wanted to convert the area into a tourist destination. But the eurocentric myth spread that "Rastafarians were going wild and killing policeman"!

Leonard Percival Howell, the earliest Rastafari, a believer in Garvey's UNIA teachings of a Black King, a Black Kingdom and a Black God, outlined the evils of racism in colonial Babylon. *The Gleaner* newspaper (1934) said Rastas were 'a "dangerous cult" attempting to infiltrate Kingston'. Leonard was declared "insane".

King James Bible was the distortion that oppressed Black peoples. But those who had hope in Psalm 68: '*Princes shall come out of Egypt and Ethiopia shall soon stretch out her hands unto God*', embraced Rastafari, when it came true in Haile Selassie. Just as whites have exalted themselves as superior, so have the Rastafaris.

Emperor Haile Selassie 1, means "Might of the Holy Trinity" and he 'is the 225th descendant of the throne of David, … the oldest throne in the world', wrote Professor Monique Bedasse (2021). Known as **Ras Tafari Makonnen**, until his coronation as Haile Selassie 1. Followers were then known as Rastafaris. Professor Bedasse explained that: 'The union between David's son Solomon and the Queen of Ethiopia, Makeda (Queen of Sheba), brought about this lineage. Haile Selassie 1 became royalty because he is a descendant of Menelik 1, who is a direct descendant of King Solomon'.

Haile Selassie's royal title is: **By the Conquering Lion of the Tribe of Judah, His Imperial Majesty Haile Selassie 1, King of Kings, Lord of Lords, Elect of God,** fulfilling the Biblical prophecy of a Black King, prophesised by Marcus Garvey decades earlier. The truth is that: "Babylon", 'ignore[d] the line of David because it provides a blatant link to Africa', according to K.P. Naphtali (1999). Nyahbinghi Order, Bobo Shanti (Ashanti), and Twelve Tribes are three different sections of Rastafari.

Rasta Symbolism of red, gold and green are the official colours of the Ethiopian Empire's Solomonic dynasty since the 17th century, according to the experts. The "Lion", represents, the 'Conquering Lion of Judah' and the "Dreads", represents the lion's mane. Rastafaris have not only developed their own language, and Rastafarianised Jamaica but have also Africanised Christianity.

Jah	From Jehovah; Living God; Haile Selassie I as the Black messiah and rebirth of Christ; God as Man; often said as "Jah Rasta Fari"
I and I	You and I; Jah is with me always; replaces the divisive pronouns, you, me we, they, etc., with communal I and I;
Babylon	modern global society; all white European organisations and institutions; downpressors (oppressors) of Black peoples
Zion	The symbolic name for Africa; Africa as the promised land, particularly Ethiopia; physical or a spiritual return to Africa
Ital	Vegetarian diet; avoidance of pork, alcohol and shellfish; emphasis on growing and eating natural food;
Dreadlocks	Hair is worn uncombed and not cut as in the Nazarite order; against Babylon's definition of white beauty; also called "natty dreads"
Reasonings	Sustained discussions; deep communal thinking; preaching down violence; "overstanding" as opposed to "understanding"

Rastafaris say that, "You can tek us out of Africa but yun cyaan't tek Africa out of us".

How did the past meet the present in music?

Image 78: Millie Small performing in Helsinki, Finland in December 1964

All attempts at cultural annihilation by white slavers failed. Matthew "Monk" Lewis (1834) a British plantation slaver said, that he had headaches because the: 'Eboes . . . roared and screamed and shouted and thumped their drums'!

Ashanti-style Burru heavy drumming: is *the* component of Jamaican music. Work songs, were 'driven on the strong beat of the digging song which helped to survive the monotony of long hours with the pick-axe', said the experts.

Mento: Jamaica's first popular modern music, combined US blues, African burru drumming and British musical elements (brass bands, sea shanties). A popular Mento song is *"Hill and Gully Rider"*, (Jamaica 55 n.d.), a call and response song.

Ska: Mento merged into ska, matching the independence mood from Britain. It was a 'bouncy sound, full of horns on top of a mento riddim', with 'influences from R&B, jazz' and with 'a faster tempo', said musicologist, Stephen Foehr (2000).

"My Boy Lollipop", by Millicent Small who was "not so small", as *The Gleaner* (2006) puts it, was the first female Jamaican ska singer to reach international fame. 'The daughter of an overseer on a sugar plantation', wrote NLJ Biographies, who sold 'over seven million copies worldwide and topped the British charts in the 60s'. Ironically, British white skinhead and punk fans were devoted ska followers. British white groups such as Madness evolved their own ska style called 2Tone (SAGE 2019).

Rocksteady: ska slowed down to match the aging audience. Singer Alton Ellis had hits with *"Rocksteady"* and 1967's *"Tougher Than Tough"*. Rocksteady linked with the Jamaican "Rude Bwoy (boy)" era of downtown's dispossessed "Yardie" culture, in Kingston's shanty towns e.g., Trench Town, Tivoli Gardens.

Sound systems: the poor could not afford uptown Kingston dances, so massive amplifiers and wardrobe-sized speakers took to the streets. Sound engineer crews, exclusive records known as "Dubplates", Selectors (deejays) and "toasters" (talking over dubplates that evolved into US rap), led to the dispossessed becoming entrepreneurs. They supplied food, alcohol and charged admission. Selectors such as 'Clement "Coxsone" Dodd, . . . became "innovative record producers", according to Paul Kauppila (2006). Innovators, 'King "Tubby" Ruddock and Lee "Scratch" Perry, who created the Dubstyle', had 'a substantial impact . . . in Western pop and electronic dance music', according to SAGE (2019).

Sound Clashes were musical battles between two or more mobile sound systems. Jamaica pioneered the concept of remixing because whoever had the best "Dubplate" could draw crowds in their thousands.

Dancehall or Bashment, focuses on bass guitars **'that echoes like a seismic tremor in your gut'** (Norman Stolzoff 2002), and "toasting" in Patois over a faster riddim, e.g., Beenie Man, Lady Saw, Yellowman. This contrasts to earlier roots reggae, by its conspicuous consumption. From higglers to Dancehall Queens, "mashing up di place" means wearing the least amount of clothing and showing off new "wine" dance moves. But, "Dancehall Queens" and "Swaggerific" men, as Khytie K Brown (2018) puts it, are criticised for its ostentatious bodily displays, dance movements, and un-Christian lyrics.

The truth is, that "Dancehall Queens" and "Swaggerific Men" can 'reimagine themselves and their circumstances innovatively', said Khytie K Brown (2018), because the historical processes left Jamaica, 'riddled with colonial, imperial, capitalist conquests', that 'fuelled community violence, economic, cultural and social degradation, and . . . trauma'. Brown believes: 'they have shunned the terror of an alienating existence and have chosen a life that is worth living in Dancehall'.

Who were the Rudies and Yardies?

Image 79: Above: Trench Town Signage. Below: Poster for The Harder They Come film starring singer, Jimmy Cliff as a Rude boy.

After abolition, structural racism by whites, continued to discriminate against the mass of Black people. But the descendants of captives, the Black peasantry and the Maroons living away from the whites in the mountains and hills, 'swelled [Kingston] in their tens of thousands', said Dr Jérémie K. Dagnini (2018). 'Bringing with them their resistance and rebellious attitudes towards Babylon', he further explained. Most became known as **Rudies** or **Yardies**.

The movement of rural to urban landless poor peasants were 'packed in overcrowded slums, ... such as **Trench Town** where reggae superstar Bob Marley was raised', wrote Dr Dagnini (2018). Described as, 'one-room huts constructed from packing cases and fish barrels of Muss, cardboard, and polythene and having few public amenities ...', said Dr Colin Clarke (1966).

Trench Town was not named by the squalid trenches in the area. But as **Trench Pen**, a thirty-three-acre cattle estate owned by Irish William Trench's son, **Daniel Trench** (1813-1884), as shown by Christopher Whyms-Stone (2005). The truth is, plots of land were given to the British when they defeated the Spaniards, leaving the mass of Black population landless at emancipation.

Trench Town has been 'identified as the birthplace of reggae, which drew its roots from ska, [and] rocksteady', wrote John Vilanova (2019). **"Sufferation"** was rampant in Trench Town; abandoned by the colonial white government; taken over by political violence with its roots in enslavement and colonialism, but immortalised by combining ska and rocksteady, called **Reggae**.

The legendary Toots and the Maytals released '*Do the Reggay*', in 1968, and popularised the word reggae, meaning *rege-rege*, (scruffy clothing or argument). 'Reggae music and the Rastafari movement were therefore borne out of [Sufferation] ... everyday life in the ghettos ...', wrote Professor Kevon Rhiney (2012).

New political rivalry co-opted the shanty town youth into the "ordinariness of everyday violence" as the past met the present. Manifesting in: 'Ghetto youth [who were] more **aggressive or ruder than ever** ... it gave birth to the **rude boy culture** ...', said music specialist Dr. Jérémie K. Dagnini (2011). He explained that: 'Rocksteady, allowed "Rude Boys"... to **sing messages of revolt**'; to **"bun fiyah"** (burn fire) as Khytie K Brown (2018) puts it, as well as **"chant down Babylon"**.

Professor Erin Mackie (2005) clarified that: 'Rudies perpetuate ... the armed desperado, with his glamorised violence, personal stature, territorialism, and bravado'. Also called "Yardies", who were the "wild west gun fighters of the Caribbean", she said. White supremacy ensured low Black ownership of land, labour and capital. Hence, Rudies were described as: 'acting like the Port Royal buccaneers pirates of the past, because, it offered "prestige"; with the reality that life, as descendants of former enslaved, Rudies' life has too few chances for betterment'.

"*The Harder They Come*" (1973) film, starred Jimmy Cliff, who acted as the rural to urban Rudie. This film's entirely reggae soundtrack and songs are preserved in the National Recording Registry and considered significant by the Library of Congress (*Jamaica-Gleaner.com* 2021). Cliff's title track and the seminal, "*Many Rivers to Cross*", has been covered by many popular artistes. Furthermore, "*Burnin*", by The Wailers, in 2007 was the first reggae album to be preserved as well.

Why has reggae gone global?

We likkle but we tallawah, as Jamaicans say, meaning, we're small, but we're mighty. With a population of less than three million, Jamaica has produced a truly staggering number of recordings relative to its population size. The "jerkiness" of reggae is captivating and infectious because, according to SAGE (2019); reggae drummers innovatively play the "one drop" pattern and is uniquely Jamaican.

Superstar Honourable Robert Nesta Marley, was an outstanding Jamaican Rastafari. Born in Nine Miles, in the hills of St Ann's parish in a humble home, (a mausoleum); raised in the government yards of Trench Town (cultural tourist hotspot), and lived in a Kingston mansion (a museum); and recorded in Tuff Gong Studios, (a museum).

Image 80: The Honourable Robert Nesta Marley

Bob Marley is legendary because, together with The Wailers, he depicted the everyday political, economic and social struggles for millions of people after de-colonisation. Marley has won many awards, toured the world and globalised Reggae and Rasta beliefs. Every February, is celebrated as Reggae Month (his birth month) and every 1 July is International Reggae Day. He was honoured with the **Order of Merit (OM)**.

'Rastafaris gave reggae music the spiritual energy to cover nearly every corner of the world', as Professor Molefi Asante (2005) has shown. 'Openness to change', was the universal value amongst reggae fans in eleven different countries, (Prof. Gail Ferguson 2016). Specifically, "conscious" or "roots" type reggae; lyrics preaching truths, rights, fighting for justice and equality and singing messages of salvation, e.g., Marley quotes from Marcus Garvey, in his prophetic *Redemption Song.*

However, Bob Marley did not invent Reggae; reggae artists are not all Rastafaris; not everyone with "Dreads" are Rastafaris and reggae does not all sound the same. It evolved into Dub (drum and bass); Dancehall (Sean Paul); Dancehall Pop (Rihanna's "Work" 2016) Ragamuffin; Ragga reggae; Lover's Rock (Black Britons); Rasta nyabinghi "Burru" drumming; Reggaetón (Spanish-speaking areas), Brazilian samba-reggae and has influenced US Rap, amongst many other genres.

The impact of reggae and Rastafaris on the worldwide cultural universe, is colossal because of its universal messages of militancy, rebelliousness and spiritual unity, as Jérémie Dagnini (2011) has shown. Reggae delivers powerful messages of hope. **It is remarkable that the descendants of oppressed people, with their ingenuity and will to survive and achieve, translated into the phenomenally creative Jamaicans,** concluded Dr Molefi Asante (2005). Furthermore, Jamaica pioneered the annual week-long Reggae Sumfest festival which attracts millions and is replicated globally.

Yet, the truth is that Jamaica, 'has not reaped the financial rewards of its cultural impact, and that's what the island really needs', said BBC Radio 6 Music presenter Don Letts. Reggae is worth US$14.5 billion, while Jamaica does not even realise US$0.5 billion of that amount, admitted John Aarons (1999) from the Recording Industry Association of America.

In 2007, Trench Town was protected by JNHT, as a Cultural Yard Heritage Site for tourists. In 2015, Kingston was designated by UNESCO as a Creative City of Music, the birthplace of mento, ska, reggae, rocksteady, dub and dancehall. In 2018, Reggae music has been added to the UNESCO Intangible Cultural Heritage, which may aid Jamaica in gaining financial rewards from their innovations and creativities by the descendants of enslaved Africans, in the future.

Why smile at the ackee tree?

Breadfruit was brought into Jamaica from Tahiti around 1793. The truth is that, the British experimented with "cheap food" by 'forcing enslaved, poor and other needy people to eat … alternative foodstuffs', wrote historian Anya Zilberstein (2016) including Britain's wretched poor. This attitude eventually evolved into the UK's "national welfare state".

Breadfruit was one of the cheapest food experiments for Jamaica, particularly in the 1780s when 'roughly 20,000 Jamaican slaves died from famine … due to bad weather, [hurricanes] poor harvests, [and US] embargos', said Anya Zilberstein (2016). But other historians believe 15,000 died. Breadfruit 'had to be transplanted from Tahiti by Captain Bligh as seedling trees'. On the way back, his own crew rebelled and the plants were left "floating around the Pacific". This was the epic Mutiny on the Bounty incident that has been made into Hollywood films.

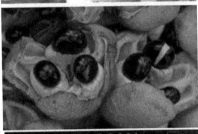

The second voyage succeeded with '1650 plants including nankas (jackfruit)', said Andrew David (1993). Other plants were 'custard apple, avocado, cabbage tree, ackee, wild mangosteen, naseberry', according to botanist, Professor Richard A Howard (1953).

Ackee, the National Fruit, grows on trees but only Jamaicans cook it as a vegetable. It grows wild, comes from North Ghana, and originally named "Ankye", from the Twi language of Ghana. Its scientific name is *Blighia sapida*, brought to Jamaica by Captain Bligh or on slaving vessels. Ackee is loaded with fibre, protein and vitamin C. It is the yellow fleshy part that is eaten.

Image 81: Above: Breadfruit. Middle: Ripe Ackee. Below: A dumpling, yam, seasoned ackee and banana breakfast in Island Village, Ocho Rios.

Eurocentrics say that it looks like scrambled eggs, when cooked. Ackee is immortalised in a folksong called, *Mi carry mi ackee go a Linstead Market*. This famous song tells of a higgler in Linstead Market who cannot sell her ackee on a Saturday night, which is the most profitable night of the week.

But the truth is that ackee is poisonous, containing a highly toxic peptide called *hypoglycin*. The US banned it in 1973, until canned or frozen ackee was produced. If eaten from the tree before smiling, it produces Jamaican vomiting sickness. In very rare cases, seizures can happen. So, ackees must only be picked when the fruit begins to smile. That is, once the skin turns red and cracks open, exposing the yellow flesh and black seeds, it "smiles". So, smiling at the fruits helps them to ripen, according to the folk tale.

Salted fish was another source of cheap food given to the enslaved. Dr Peter Pellizzari's 1752-1769 research (2020), showed that Jamaica imported 25 million pounds of fish (cod) with 14.4 million from New England, US before the 1776 war. 'Ireland was a significant source of salted provisions such as beef, pork, butter, and fish', he said. Salted fish was combined with ackee, as ackee alone 'cannot provide a 'bellyful', said Professor John Rashford, a Jamaican-American.

The truth is that, Ackee and Saltfish is only indigenous to Jamaica, and not any other Caribbean island. Combining this unlikely pair, is uniquely Jamaican and is now **Jamaica's national dish.** It is often served with roasted breadfruit. Together with Jamaican spices and peppers it is usually eaten as the "national breakfast", but also as snacks, for lunch or dinner.

From the days of enslavement, 'the "lowly ackee and saltfish", now tops the list of the island's favourite dishes', according to Dr Rashford. Today, 'ackee export earnings averaged about US $15 million annually', said Debbian Wray (2020).

What is the jerk in jerk chicken?

Described as hoghunters of forest swines, the maroons adopted the Taínos 'technique of slow-cooking hog meat over a smoky wood fire', (*The Sunday Gleaner* 2014). Fire and smoke could not be used or they risked revealing their mountainous locations to the British forces, so underground pits were used.

Image 82: Rastafari cooking Jerk chicken in jerk pan at Notting Hill Carnival, London. As Rastas avoid pork, chicken has become the favourite meat for jerking.

Today, Montego Bay is a 20-mile tourist hotspot, (Maroons Cockpit Country of the past). But it was once known as *Bahía de Mantega*, meaning "hog's butter" or "pig's lard", and where the Spanish 'killed 80,000 hogs every year for the sake of their grease'. These hogs roamed Cockpit Country; so hunting the boars became a 'favourite diversion of the Maroons', as noted by John Stewart in 1808, a colonist who lived in Jamaica for twenty-one years.

John Smith (1823) described the barbecued pig as 'a great delicacy ... being the hog's flesh smoked with a certain odoriferous wood, which communicates to it a peculiar flavour'. Matthew "Monk" Lewis (1834) a British absentee slaver said that, 'barbecued pig', was the 'best and richest dish that I ever tasted'. Probable usage of the word 'jerk' came from the Taíno word *"ch'arki"*. But the truth is, any links between *ch'arki* and Jamaican Jerk are unconvincing and may only lie in the English corruption of *ch'arki*. In true Maroon fashion, jerked meat is:

Jerking meat originated exclusively in Jamaica

- marinading, seasoning any meat or fish, in Jamaican peppers, spices, pimentos
- wrapped in plaintain leaves or green branches from the pimento trees
- the marinade is 'jerked' though the holes and cooked by steam
- buried in an underground pit, filled with hot stones, and cooked by vapours for many hours

... the wild swines ... [are] cut open, the bones taken out, the flesh is gashed on the inside into the skin, filled with salt, and exposed to the sun, which is called jerking. Quote 37: *Phillip Henry Gosse (1851)*

After the British-Maroon Peace Treaties, Maroons no longer had to hide the smoke, Quote 37. Later, *baricoa* (barbecues) begun with lattices of pimento wood over four forked sticks above a slow fire. Then, in the 20th century, sheets of metals as griddles covered with plantain leaves were used.

Subsequently, innovative Jamaicans repurposed excesses of imported metal oil-drums. Now called jerk pans, oil-barrels were split in half, fitted with hinges and ventilation holes. Meat or fish is seasoned, marinaded, which are jerked through the holes and cooked by trapping the vapours.

Jamaican Jerk is not only uniquely Jamaican and delicious, but also a style of seasoning and marinading using native Jamaican spices; evolving from underground pits to barbecues to jerk-pans. Also, a national identity and a rejection of colonial oppression. To protect against mis-appropriation, the Government has **copyrighted "Jamaican Jerk"** in 2015 against imitations, along with **"Blue Mountain Coffee"** and **"Jamaica Rum"**.

The truth is that, dominant white cultures, who already have "white privileges", misappropriate, and profit from Caribbean culture. E.g., a UK's famous TV British cookery star, launched "Punchy Jerk Rice", in 2018. But the truth is, there is no jerk in the dish and rice cannot be jerked! Thus, damaging the jerk name whilst profitting from the innovations of disenfranchised Black people.

Running out of poverty!

For its small size and economic challenges, Jamaica is the **"sprint capital of the world"**, (Delano Franklyn 2010) and has given birth to some of the fastest runners history has ever known.

1. Donald Quarrie (ten golds between 1970; 1984)
2. Merlene Ottey (six golds between 1979; 1995)
3. Shelly Ann Fraser-Pryce (18 golds in 2008; 2012; 2020)
4. Sherone Simpson (one Olympic gold 2004, ten golds)
5. Veronica Campbell Brown (3 golds 2004; 2008; 24 golds)
6. **Usain 'Lightning' Bolt - (23 golds; 100m world record in 2009)**
7. Yohan Black (two golds 2012, 2016 and 16 golds)

Image 83: Usain Bolt's Tracks & Records restaurant on Hip Strip and Statute, in Montego Bay, Jamaica

Why Jamaican sprinters are so fast and have an unparalleled record of international success, appear to be issues for eurocentrics. The truth is that, no "speed gene" is responsible. If speed is in the genes, that means: 'Jamaicans had little to do with their own athletic success', according to Jamaican-American Dr Sasha Turner (2016); essentially the, "extraordinary Negro stereotype" of previous eras.

British sports were introduced to "discipline" colonised people, as Dr Turner has shown. Since then, Jamaica remains the world champion in cricket and in athletics. Generations of Jamaicans saw Britain as their "mother country" and flocked to British sports to debunk the so-called "uncivilised" and "inferior" white myths. It was also an inexpensive way out of poverty. Dr Turner said that: 'Driven to prove self-worth, masculinity, and strength, Jamaican boys and girls practised tirelessly and barefooted in the streets and yards and competed fiercely in interscholastic games'.

Genetics: It's symmetry! "those with the most symmetrical knees have the best times', concluded Professor Robert Trivers (2013). But which came first? Symmetrical knees with or without years of training? The truth is that, there is no proven evidence, and white supremacists may demand segregation as "fairer" competition if due to genetic advantages.

Facilities: It's the wealth of world-class trained coaches and sporting facilities! Jamaican athletes have the finest coaching from infancy. It's 'the actual grass in fields that Jamaican pickney a run pon from the time them likkle bit', said sociologist, Nazma Muller (2012), and thus, when running on 'official tracks, they're even faster'.

British Slave Trade: It's survival of the fittest! Survivors of the Atlantic crossing death trap, meant that the, 'fittest slaves survived', asserted Professor William Aiken (2006). It was the 'modification to the genetic and metabolic profiles of those who arrived, ... making them better able to function when oxygen is deficient'. Thus, 'the strongest, most resilient and determined lived. Hence their legendary fighting spirit', believes Nazma Muller (2012). But there is no evidence for this.

Nutrition: It's the yam and green banana! Both staple crops and eaten from young. Evidence shows that they provide a metabolic boost when needed. But these foods are not exclusively Jamaican. Although, Jamaica's heavy plant-based diet, from Rastafari, called *Ital,* has become embedded and may have some impact, *Ital* food cannot be overlooked.

Role Models: 'It's culture not genetics!', concluded Orville Taylor (2015). Youngsters have a 'pantheon of track stars and icons', for aspiration. This 'creates a strong socialising impact', because, 'success breed success'.

Character: It's the Jamaican inner strength, and resilience! 'Running was resistance', and past daily life involved the 'spirit of the sprint ... uphill, across valleys, byways and highways', as Sir Hilary Beckles (2019) has highlighted.

The truth is, what began as "contesting the Black uncivilised and white civilised myth" of the colonisers, Jamaicans had and continue to, **"repurposed that myth into world-class international Jamaican sports people of today"**.

Chapter 12

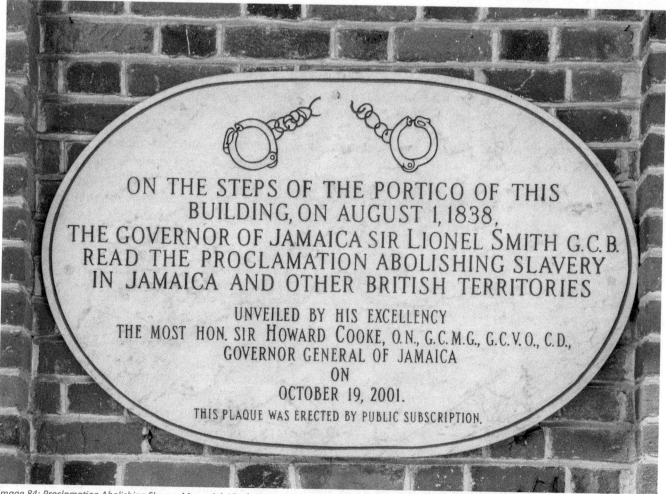

Image 84: Proclamation Abolishing Slavery Memorial, King's House, Main Square, Spanish Town, Saint Catherine Parish, Jamaica

What is reparatory justice?

- "the making of amends for wrong or injury done", (Oxford Dictionary)
- "giving satisfaction for a wrong or injury ", (Merriam-Webster.com)
- "a symbolic way of accounting for a society's past wrongdoing", (Professors Luke Moffett and others 2018)

Image 85: CARICOM means Caribbean Community and Common Market. Founded in 1973 and consists of twenty Caribbean countries.

Reparations for the legacy of: 'Indigenous genocide, African chattel slavery and genocide, and Asian contract slavery ... by which the British state forcefully extracted wealth from the Caribbean resulting in its persistent, endemic poverty', stated Professor Sir Hilary Beckles, Vice-chancellor of UWI, addressing the UK Parliament on Reparations in 2014.

Reparations is *not* about money! However, in 2014, Dorbrene E. O'Marde, Chairperson of the Antigua and Barbuda Reparations Support Commission, highlighted past European reparations that paid out:

- 'a sum of twenty million pounds was paid to enslavers',
- 'in 1815 [Britain] paid Portugal £750,000 to restrict the trade to Brazil';
- 'in 1817 [Britain] paid Spain £400,000 to abandon the trade to Cuba, Puerto Rico, and Santo Domingo'.

In more modern times:

- 'sixty billion dollars so far and running' to the Jews ... for the holocaust in Nazi Germany',
- 'the Maoris in New Zealand received $160 million and a large expanse of territory', in 2006 (Britain).
- '$20,000 and a letter of apology from President Bush', to the Japanese after WW2, (Allan D. Cooper 2012).
- Poland demanded $284 million plus lands and concessions from Germany for using Poles as slave labour.

The Jamaican Parliament called for reparations to the United Kingdom for crimes against humanity in 2009. Lord Anthony Gifford QC, a British hereditary peer, senior barrister and expert on international law, wrote:

> [W]hy do the peoples of the Caribbean suffer racial discrimination and racial disadvantage? It is because the UK ... committed crimes against humanity against their ancestors and have never paid a penny of compensation. What is the remedy? It is in the [CARICOM] Ten Point Action Plan, which can also be seen as an outline of a negotiating strategy, (in Dorbrene E O'Marde 2019).

Reparation as justice for Africans that suffered under chattel slavery, colonialism and post colonialism must include; acknowledgement; responsibility and remedy. These include official apologies; not vague wordings, nor regrets that only serve white absolution. To include heritage projects, memorials, and educational initiatives, museums, commemorations and return of stolen artefacts. The focus must be on Black peoples' achievement and agency rather than the 'white saviour brigade'. However, eurocentric historians, white supremacists and white experts claim that:

-It was a long time ago; slavery was "legal" at the time;
-Genocide was not illegal until after 1940s;
-Nobody is alive now who experienced the British slave trade;
-Official apologies may have legal outcomes;
-Some Black people are successful and wealthy today;
-No single group benefitted exclusively from slavery;

-Reparation claims are just desperate begging
-No direct link between enslavement and racism;
-Caribbean political leaders are incompetence and corrupt;
-My/our ancestors did not own slaves;
-Not all Africans/Jamaicans suffered under slavery;
-Some whites fought against slavery;

Yet the truth is, behind the "illusions" of white excuses, the root cause of Jamaica's endemic issues, is that Jamaica 'still has to confront the legacies of centuries of slavery, colonial dominance, economic exploitation, and racial-cultural categorisation of its population', said Professor Claudia Rauhut (2018). This is because 'little or no attempt was made by the authorities to erect in its place [enslavement] a properly designed and well-founded social structure', argued Hugh Paget (1945) after emancipation. **The British Parliament left no one who knew how to run a government or maintain it!** Thus: **'Reparations is not about money, charity or begging but about solving the mess that the British left behind and walked away from in 1962 ... that trade [which] helped Britain to industrialise and develop',** as Sir Beckles has shown.

Moving outta Babylon and stepping into Zion?

The CARICOM Reparations Commission (CRC) composes of academics, lawyers, and other civil society activists from twenty former Caribbean colonies. They have put forward a Ten-Point Action Plan as shown. Repatriation is point two.

Reparations is: 'Redressing past wrongs [which] is essential to establishing conditions of justice in a society scarred by the enduring and pervasive effects of those wrongs', said Professor Emeritus of Philosophy, Thomas McCarthy (2004), because:

> At its height, British Empire ships carried more slaves than any other nation, their slave colonies produced vast quantities of tropical goods, and the country as a whole grew rich on the profits of African slavery. (Professor, John R. Oldfield, Southampton University (2012).

CARICOM TEN POINT ACTION PLAN

1. Full formal apology
2. Repatriation for those who desire it
3. Indigenous peoples' development programme
4. Building of cultural institutions
5. Tackling chronic diseases
6. Eradication of illiteracy
7. African knowledge programme
8. Psychological rehabilitation
9. Technological transfer and science sharing
10. Debt Cancellation

Rastafaris allegiance to Ethiopia (e.g., anti-Jamaica, anti-British) led to early colonial brutality until acceptance by Emperor Haile Selassie I's visit to Jamaica in 1966. Since then, the growth of Rastafari has been spectacular; spread through hundreds of roots reggae tunes, religious interpretations, political aims and self-development as Professor Giulia Bonacci (2020) has demonstrated. Repatriation theme is captured in Bob Marley's lyrics in "*Exodus*", 'most profoundly, poetically and emphatically', described Professor Michael Barnett (2019).

Professor Claudia Rauhut (2018) said: 'Rastafarians ... have repeatedly petitioned the British Queen to facilitate their repatriation to Africa as a form of reparations'. She said that, the Rastafaris presented a lawsuit for reparations to Queen Elizabeth during her Golden Jubilee tour visit to Jamaica in 2002. But 'the applicants / claimants did not provide sufficient evidence that they were indeed descendants of enslaved Africans brought to Jamaica'. Therefore, the claim was dismissed.

Since Marcus Garvey's call of "Africa for the Africans at Home and Abroad", and Rastafaris calls for reparatory justice as **"Moving outta Babylon and stepping into Zion"**, (Professor Barnett); CARICOM's Reparatory plan, includes repatriation but only for those who desire it. Some believe repatriation to be spiritual rather than a physical repatriated to "Zion", i.e., free from white oppression, from racism, from injustices and from inequalities.

The truth is that, Haile Selassie I donated land grants called Shashemene in Ethiopia for Rastafaris. Ethiopia is viewed as the Biblical Promised Land to Rastafaris, the only country in Africa that was not colonised in the "Scramble for Africa" (1885 – 1914). According to Professor Bonacci, in the mid-2000s, over 130,000 Rastafaris now live in Shashemene. Some have repatriated to other parts (Ghana, Tanzania or South Africa etc.,). Interestingly, a phenomenon of "white Rastas" also live in Shashemene. Dr Bennett identified these non-Black Rastas as "Euro-Americans, British, Swedish, German, French, Austrian and even Italians ... who unabashedly consider themselves as Rastafari settlers in Ethiopia"!

A symbolic repatriation occurred in 1998. According to UNESCO (2009), four skeletal remains from house-yard burials in Seville Heritage Park (St Ann's parish) were excavated and taken to USA for analysis. With government agreements, one of those four skeletal remains resulted in repatriation back to Ghana. This repatriation of one skeletal remains symbolically represented **all the enslaved Africans**, returning back to their original homeland.

Professor Sir Hilary Beckles, in his speech in the House of Commons on 16 July 2014, declared that: '**This 21st century will be the century of global reparatory justice**'.

A *few sincere reparatory apologies*

- "In the course of history, men belonging to Christian nations did not always do this, and we ask pardon from our African brothers who suffered so much because of the trade in [B]lacks". **Pope John Paul II. 14 August 1985**

- "We apologise to the millions of African sons and daughters kidnapped directly from the continent who suffered profound physical and mental abuse. This is at the heart of our apology". **Liverpool City, UK. December 1999.**

- "We profoundly regret the injustices of the past". **Juan Carlos Aparicio (Spain).** Spanish Labour and Social Affairs Minister, said of African slavery. **1 September 2001**. World Conference Against Racism. South Africa.

- "We express deep remorse about enslavement and the slave trade". "It is important to implement structural measures that benefit the descendants of former slaves and future generations". Dutch, **Roger Van Boxtel, 4 September 2001**. Netherlands:

- "Please forgive us if in any way we contributed to what you had to suffer". **Ghanaian Archbishop Charles G. Palmer-Buckle, National Catholic Reporter, 13 September 2002**. Ghana has developed "Project Joseph", after the Biblical Joseph who sold his brothers into slavery, to welcome those in the diasporas to visit, emigrate, own land, invest, and start businesses.

- "I have said we are sorry and I say it again … [It is important] to remember what happened in the past, to condemn it and say why it was entirely unacceptable". **Tony Blair, March 2007** (UK Prime Minister 1997- 2007). After refusing to apologise in 2001.

- "As mayor, I offer an apology on behalf of London and its institutions for their role in the transatlantic slave trade". **Ken Livingstone, Mayor of London. August 2007**. A 'tearful expression of remorse' was noted.

- "Today, without equivocation, we apologise for what occurred in Coral Gardens. We express our regret and sorrow for this chapter in our national life that was characterised by brutality, injustice and repression, which was wrong and should never be repeated." **Andrew Holness. Current Jamaican Prime Minister. 4 April 2017**. A Rastafari cultural centre, heritage status and trust fund of J$ 10-million to pay reparations to the survivors of the incident.

- "the sugar industry on which both the Tate and the Lyle firms … was itself absolutely constructed on the foundation of slavery in the 17th and 18th centuries, both in supply and in demand. Without slavery, the British sugar industry … would not have existed … it is therefore not possible to separate the Tate galleries from the history of colonial slavery". **Tate.org. August 2019**.

- "We are sorry for the role played by the Lloyd's market in the 18th and 19th Century slave trade – an appalling and shameful period of English history". **Lloyd's of London. 10 June 2020**. Started by Edward Lloyd in 1688, now a commercial insurance giant.

- "eighteenth and nineteenth century slave trade was an unacceptable part of British history. [B]ut we are aware of some inexcusable connections involving former Governors and Directors, and apologise for them". Statement from the **Bank of England. 19 June 2020**. Includes four of UK's largest banks, Barclays, HSBC, Lloyds and the NatWest Group.

- "In 2006 the General Synod of the Church of England issued an apology, acknowledging the part the Church itself played in historic cases of slavery. It is a source of shame that others within the Church actively perpetrated slavery and profited from it". **Church of England. 19 June 2020**.

- Councillor Alistair Sinclair said: "Slavery was the foundation on which the industrial revolution was built and paid for many of the Georgian buildings of Lancaster and many subsequent Victorian industrial buildings". **Lancaster City Council. 1 July 2020**.

- "93 of the National Trust's stately country buildings have direct links to colonialism and slavery including UK Prime Minister, Winston Churchill's home (during WW2)". "[T]he proceeds of foreign conquest and the slavery economy built and furnished houses and properties, endowed the families who kept them", **National Trust for Places of Historic Interest. September 2020**.

- "It is inexcusable that one of our founders profited from slavery and while that was nearly 200 years ago we can't pretend it didn't happen". **Greene King. 1 October 2020**. Founded in 1799, with pubs called *"The Black Boy"* and *"The Black's Head"*.

- "We are deeply sorry that the origins of our endowment have roots in shameful practices that caused deep suffering and created enduring harms". **Board of Trustees, The Rowntree Society. 15 Apr 2021** (confectionary, chocolates and sweet companies).

- "Sir Robert Clayton was a principal member of the Royal Africa Company, a corporation that forcibly transported 44,000 Africans across the Atlantic … and president of St Thomas's Hospital". Thomas Guy investment in the South Sea Company, netted "£424.7 million in 2020 values". He used that money to fund Guy's Hospital. Labels stating links with enslavement will be put on Clayton and Guy's statutes. **Guys & St Thomas Hospital Foundation. 1 September 2021**.

RFERENCES CITED

Chapter 1

- Sandra W Meditz, Dennis M. Hanratty, Library of Congress (1989) *Islands of the Commonwealth Caribbean: ….* Washington, D.C. Federal Research
- JIS (8 November 2019) *PHOTOS: Launch of Public Petition for the Granting of Official Status to the Jamaican Language.* https://jis.gov.jm/photos-launch-of-public-petition-for-the-granting-of-official-status-to-the-jamaican-language/
- Richard S Dunn (1972) From Sugar and Slaves: The Rise of the Planter Class in the English West Indies, 1624-1713. *Omohundro Institute of Early American History and Culture.* University of North Carolina Press
- NLJ (n.d.) History Notes. Information on Jamaica's Culture & Heritage. *History of Hurricanes & Floods.* https://nlj.gov.jm/history-notes-jamaica/
- Wendy A Lee (2009) History of Jamaica. *In Lesley-Gail Atkinson ed. (2006) The earliest inhabitants: The dynamics of the Jamaican Taíno* UWI
- National Archives Gov. Colonial Office and predecessors: Jamaica, Original Correspondence. https://discovery.nationalarchives.gov.uk/details/r/C4328
- World Atlas (February 25, 2021) North America: Maps: Jamaica. https://www.worldatlas.com/maps/jamaica
- JIS (no date) Parish Profiles. Overview of Jamaica. Jamaica Information Service. https://jis.gov.jm/information/parish-profiles/
- Worldometers.info (2021) *Jamaica:* Published in Dover, Delaware, U.S.A.
- United Nations by Pedro Conceição (2019) *Human Development Report 2019: beyond income, beyond averages, beyond today: inequalities in human development in the 21st century.* United Nations Development Programme.
- World Health Organization (2018) WHO country cooperation strategy at a glance: Jamaica. *World Health Organisation.* https://apps.who.int/iris/handle/10665/136900.
- Carolyn Cooper *In* Charlie Pittock (22 Sept 2021) Queen on brink after Jamaica say it's 'time to get rid' of monarch as head of state. *Express.co.uk* https://www.express.co.uk/news/royal/1494554/queen-elizabeth-ii-jamaica-monarch-head-of-state-royal-family-spt
- Nadine Hunt (2010) Expanding the Frontiers of Western Jamaica through Minor Atlantic …: *Canadian Journal of History;* 45(3) 485 ProQuest One
- Encyclopedia Britannica (6 February 2020) Middlesex. *Encyclopedia Britannica.* https://www.britannica.com/place/Middlesex-historical-county
- The World Factbook (25 February 2021) Washington, DC: *Central Intelligence Agency/.* https://www.cia.gov/the-world-factbook/countries/jamaica/
- Andrew Wheatley (Sunday, January 10, 2021) Portmore 15: Parish formation in Jamaica — A short history: *Jamaica Observer Newspaper*
- JNHT (2011) *Edinburgh Castle.* http://www.jnht.com/site_edinburgh_castle.php
- JNHT (2011) *Colbeck Castle.* http://www.jnht.com/site_colbeck_castle.php
- NLJ (no date) *Quick References: Place names in Jamaica* and *History Notes: Information on Jamaica's Culture & Heritage*
- NLJ (no date) Resource Guides: *Handbook of Jamaica:*
- UNESCO: Blue and John Crow Mountains: (2015) World Heritage List: *UNESCO. https://whc.unesco.org/en/list/1356/*
- World Atlas (11 November 2020) North America: Maps of Jamaica https://www.worldatlas.com/maps/jamaica
- The World Factbook (25 February 2021) Washington, DC: *Central Intelligence Agency/*
- Jamaica Cave Register (2020) R. S. Stewart: *Jamaican Caves Organisation*
- Rev William R.F. McGhie (2014) Story of the flags. http://www.flagupscotjam.uk/story-of-the-flags/
- Patrick Allen (n.d.) Governor-General's Message for National Heritage Week. https://kingshouse.gov.jm/speech/governor-generals-message-for-national-heritage-week/
- NLJ (no date) Quick References: *Jamaican National Symbols.* https://nlj.gov.jm/story-jamaican-national-flag/
- JIS (14 August 2013) *Symbols: Description of the Doctor Bird* https://jis.gov.jm/information/symbols/jamaican-national-bird-the-doctor-bird/
- Steve O. Buckridge (2003) The Role of Plant Substances in Jamaican Slave Dress, *Caribbean Quarterly,* 49:3, 61-73
- David Northrup (1976) The Compatibility of the Slave and Palm Oil Trades in the Bight of Biafra. *The Journal of African History,* v17(3) 353–364
- Tania Mott (2016) Compensation to landowners for use of bauxite lands in Jamaica: … *Commonwealth Law Bulletin,* 42:2, 161-180
- Claremont Kirton, and James Ferguson (1992) *Jamaica Debt and Poverty.* Oxfam GB
- Jamaica Bauxite Institute (2018) World Production of Bauxite. World Ranking: *United States Geological Survey.*
- Neil MacDonald (1990) The Caribbean: Making our own choices. *Oxfam GB*
- JEB - Jamaica Tourist Board (2019) *Visitor Arrivals to Jamaica (Annual) 2006 to 2020*
- IPCC - Intergovernmental Panel on Climate Change's (2007) Climate change 2007: Synthesis report …: *Intergovernmental Panel on Climate Change*
- NEPA (2011) State of the Environment Report 2010. Kingston: *The National Environment and Planning Agency*

Chapter 2

- William Keegan (2019) *Insular Caribbean Early Settlers of the Dearchaizing the Archaic* edited by Sidestone Press
- James Lee (1976) Jamaican Redware. *Archaeology Jamaica* 76, no. 2: 1–5.
- David Burley et al (2017) Jamaican Taíno Settlement Configuration at the Time of Christopher Columbus. *Latin American Antiquity,* v28(3) 337-352
- Lesley-Gail Atkinson ed. (2006) *The earliest inhabitants: The dynamics of the Jamaican Taíno.* University of West Indies Press
- Jorge Estevez, Rene Perez Liciaga (2016) Origins of the word Taíno. http://www.openanthropology.org/resurgence/hispaniola.htm
- Basil Reid (2009) *Myths and Realities of Caribbean History.* The University of Alabama Press. *Project MUSE* muse.jhu.edu/book/6789
- L. Antonio Curet (2014). The Taíno: Phenomena, Concepts, and Terms. Ethnohistory. 61. 467-495
- Hilaire Kallendorf (1995) A Myth Rejected: The Noble Savage in Dominican Dystopia. *Journal of Latin American Studies,* v27(2) 449–470
- Minority Rights Group International, (2008) World Directory of Minorities and Indigenous Peoples - Dominica: Caribs; https://www.refworld.org/
- Lisa Hendry, National History Museum (NHM) (no date) *https://www.nhm.ac.uk/discover/the-cannibals-of-goughs-cave.html*
- *Encyclopedia Britannica* (6 August 2019) Carib. The Editors of Encyclopedia. *Encyclopedia Britannica.*
- Hilary McD. Beckles (2008) Kalinago (Carib) Resistance to European Colonisation of the Caribbean, *Caribbean Quarterly,* 54:4, 77-94
- Peter Hulme, N. Whitehead, (1992) Wild Majesty: Encounters with Caribs from Columbus to the Present Day. *In* Hilaire Kallendorf (1995) A Myth Rejected: The Noble Savage in Dominican Dystopia. *Journal of Latin American Studies,* v27(2) p 449–470
- Washington Irving [Original 1828] *The Life and Voyages of Christopher Columbus In* John Harmon McElroy (1981) (ed.) *The Complete Works of Washington Irving.* Vol. XI Boston: Twayne
- Maximilian C Forte (2006) Extinction: Ideologies Against Indigeneity in the Caribbean. *Southern Quarterly;* Summer 43(4) 46
- *Encyclopedia Britannica* (8 May 2020) Taíno. The Editors. *Encyclopedia Britannica.*
- *New World Encyclopedia* Contributors (15 January 2020) Taíno. *New World Encyclopedia.*
- *World FactBook* (25 February 2021) Jamaica: Central America. *World FactBook*
- Daniel Thwaites, (27 July 2014) Wackos are Not Extinct. *The Gleaner Newspaper*
- Hannes Schroeder et al (2018) Origins and genetic legacies of the Caribbean Taíno. *Proceedings of the National Academy of Sciences* 115.10.2341-2346
- Irving Rouse (1992) *The Taínos: Rise and Decline of the People Who Greeted Columbus.* New Haven: Yale University Press
- Joanna Ostapkowicz (2015) The Sculptural Legacy of the Jamaican Taíno: Part 1: The Carpenter's Mountain Carvings. 10.13140/RG.2.1.2613.6162.
- Marshall B. McKusick (1960) *Aboriginal canoes in the West Indies.* University Press. Department of Anthropology

Chapter 3

- National Geographic, Erin Blackmore (12 December 2019) *Who were the Moors*? https://www.nationalgeographic.com/history/article/who-were-moors
- Colin Smith, Ed (1988) Christians and Moors in Spain *In* Ross Brann (2009) "The Moors?" Medieval Encounters: *Jewish, Christian, and Muslim Culture in Confluence and Dialogue*, v15(2-4) p 307-318
- Kathleen Deagan, (2003) Colonial Origins and Colonial Transformations in Spanish America. *Historical Archaeology*. v37(4) 3–13
- Asselin Charles (1995) Colonial Discourse Since Christopher Columbus. *Journal of Black Studies*, 26(2) 134-152
- Ross Brann (2009) The Moors? Medieval Encounters: *Jewish, Christian, and Muslim Culture in Confluence and Dialogue*. v15(2-4) 307-318
- *Encyclopedia Britannica*. The Editors of Encyclopaedia (17 September 2020) Moor. *Encyclopedia Britannica*
- Josiah Blackmore (2006) Imagining the Moor in Medieval Portugal. *Diacritics*, v36(3-4) Fall-Winter 27-43
- Imtiaz Habib (2008) *Black Lives in the English Archives, 1500–1677*, Aldershot
- *Encyclopedia.com* (2021) Spanish Conquistadors. *U*X*L Encyclopedia of U.S. History*
- Carl Zimmer (2019) A History of the Iberian Peninsula, as Told by Its Skeletons. *New York times*. nytimes.com/2019/03/14/science/iberia-prehistory-dna.html
- Timothy J Yeager (1955) Encomienda or Slavery? The Spanish Crown's Choice of Labor Organization in Sixteenth-Century .... *The Journal of Economic History*.v55(4) 842–859
- UNESCO (2009) Seville Heritage Park: Tentative Lists. https://whc.unesco.org/en/tentativelists/5431/
- Encyclopedia Britannica *(2020) Christopher Columbus: Italian Explorer.* Encyclopedia Britannica
- Carla Gardina Pestana (2005) English Character and the Fiasco of the Western Design. *Early American Studies*, v3(1) 1–31
- Judith A Carney (2015) Columbian exchange. In *The Princeton Companion to Atlantic*
- Alfred W Crosby (1972) The Columbian Exchange: Biological and Cultural Consequences of 1492. *In* JA Carney (2015). Columbian exchange. In *The Princeton Companion to Atlantic History. UCLA*.
- Charles C. Mann (2012) *1493: Uncovering the New World Columbus Created: History and Philosophy of the Life Sciences*, v15(3) 313–327
- Francisco Guerra (1993) The European-American exchange." *History and philosophy of the life sciences* vol. 15,3 (1993): 313-27
- Verene Shepherd (March 2021) Environmental justice, the climate crisis and people of African descent. https://www.ohchr.org/Documents/Issues/Racism/WGEAPD/Session28/statement-vereneshepherd.pdf
- Lancashire Evening Post, Jack Marshall (18th November 2021) Facing up to Lancaster's slave-trade heritage: 'We have to be honest about our history; we can't airbrush out the bits we don't like'. *Lancashire Evening Post*, JPI Media Publishing Ltd.
- Linda A. Newson (2006) *The Pathology of Discovery and Conquest*: Gresham College
- J.M.G. Le Clézio (1988) The Mexican Dream: Chicago, *The University of Chicago Press* (Translated by Teresa Lavender Fagan
- George E Tinker, Mark Freeland (2008) Thief, Slave Trader, Murderer: Christopher Columbus and Caribbean Population Decline. *Wicazo Sa Review*, v23(1) 25-50. *Project MUSE*, doi:10.1353/wic.2008.0002.
- *Encyclopedia Britannica* (2021) E. Dussel, (27 June 2021) *Bartolomé de Las Casas. Encyclopedia Britannica*.
- Fernando Jorge Cruz Mouta (2019) Por Virtud Del Asiento: The Naval Logistics of the Slave Trade to the Spanish Indies (1604-1624). *International Journal of Maritime History*, v31(4) 707–728
- Trevor Burnard (2020) A Pack of Knaves. The Royal African Company, the Development of the Jamaican Plantation Economy ..., 1672-1708." *Journal of Colonialism & Colonial Hist*ory, v21(2)

Chapter 4

- University of Iowa, Art & Life in Africa. *Igbo Ukwu. Types of Art*. https://africa.uima.uiowa.edu/peoples/show/Igbo+Ukwu
- Gloria Chuku (2018) Igbo historiography: Parts I, II, and III. *History Compass*.16: e12489
- Emeka Okonkwo, A.M. Ibeanu (2016) Nigeria's Archaeological Heritage: Resource Exploitation and Technology. *SAGE Open*
- Stephen D Behrendt (2001) Markets, Transaction Cycles, and Profits: Merchant Decision Making in the British Slave Trade. *The William and Mary Quarterly*, v58(1) 171–204. *Omohundro Institute of Early American History and Culture*
- Douglas Chambers (2002) The Significance of Igbo in the Bight of Biafra Slave-Trade: *A Rejoinder to Northrup's 'Myth Igbo'*, 23:1, 101-120
- Simon P. Newman et al (2013) The West African Ethnicity of the Enslaved in Jamaica. *Slavery & Abolition*. v34(3) p 376-400
- James Delle (2009) ...An Archaeology of Colonial Modernity at Marshall's Pen, Jamaica. *International Journal of Historical Archaeology*, v13(4) 488–512
- Jessica Krug (2014) Social Dismemberment, Social (Re)membering: Obeah Idioms, Kromanti Identities ..., *Slavery & Abolition* 35(4) 537–58.
- Robert B. Edgerton (1995) *The Fall of the Asante Empire. The Hundred-Year War for Africa's Gold Coast*. New York
- *Encyclopedia of War*. Dennis J Cowles (2017) Jamaica. *The SAGE Encyclopedia of War: Social Science Perspectives.* SAGE Publications, p. 914-15
- Christina Griffith, (2019) The Asante Gold Weights" *Expedition Magazine* 61.2. http://www.penn.museum/sites/expedition/?p=27963
- Paul Banahene Adjei (2015) Adinkra Symbols of Ghana: *The SAGE Encyclopedia of African Cultural Heritage in North America*: SAGE Publications
- Beverley Stoeltje (1997) Asante Queen Mothers. *Annals of the New York Academy of Sciences*, v810(1) p 41-71.
- Toby Green (2019) *A fistful of shells: West Africa from the rise of the slave trade to the age of revolution*. Penguin UK
- Kwame Y. Daaku (1970) Trade and Politics on the Gold Coast, 1600-1720: *A Study of the African Reaction to European Trade* (Oxford: Clarendon)
- Rebecca Shumway (2014) The Fante Shrine of Nananom Mpow and the Atlantic .... *International Journal of African Historical Studies* 44.1(27-IV)
- Captain Robert Sutherland Rattray et al (1927) *Religion and art in Ashanti*. Clarendon Press.
- Encyclopedia of Anthropology, Mary Carol Hopkins (2006) Asante. by H. J. Birx Thousand Oaks: *SAGE Publications, Inc.* 284-93
- Amanda Logan (2020) Tasting Privilege and Privation during Asante Rule and the Atlantic Slave Trade. *The Scarcity Slot*. UCP. 61-94.
- Molefi Kete Asante, Ama Mazama (2005). Middle passage. In Encyclopedia of black studies v1, p. 331-333. SAGE Publications, Inc
- Thomas E Kyei (1992) Marriage and Divorce among the Ashanti: *A Study Undertaken in the Course of the 'Ashanti Social* Survey' 1945
- Stefano Boni (2002) The Encompassment of the Autonomous Wife. Hierarchy in Akan Marriage (Ghana). *Anthropos*, 97(1) 55-72
- New World Encyclopedia contributors, 'Fante Confederacy', *New World Encyclopedia,*, 27 May 2008.
- B. Wasserman (1961) The Ashanti War of 1900: A Study in Cultural Conflict. *Africa: Journal of the International African Institute*, *31*(2) 167-179
- Albert A Boahen & E K Akyeampong (2003) Yaa Asantewaa and the Asante-British War of 1900-1. Accra: Sub-Saharan Publishers.
- Ghana Statistical Service (2012) *2010 – Population and Housing Consensus*. Sakoa Press Ltd., Accra.
- W. F. Mitchell (2009) *African American Food Culture*. Westport, CT: Greenwood Press.
- Kwesi Anquandah (1999) Castles and Forts of Ghana. *Ghana Museums and Monuments* Board (Paris: Atalante)
- Edward Addo (2011) European heritage and cultural diversity: ..., *Journal of Contemporary African Studies*, 29:4, 405-425
- Joseph S Kaminski (2016) The Yam Festival Celebrated by the Asante People in Kumase in 1817: *Music in Art*, v41(1-2) p 95-109
- Walter Rodney (1966) African slavery and other forms of social oppression on the Upper Guinea .... *The Journal of African History*, 7(3), 431-44
- Judith Spicksley (2013) Pawns on the Gold Coast: The Rise of Asante and ... Debt, 1680–1750, *Journal of African history*, v54(2) 147-175
- Sarah Balakrishnan (2020) of Debt and Bondage: From Slavery to Prisons in the Gold Coast, c. 1807–1957. *Journal of African History*, v61(1) p 3-21

- Orlando Patterson (1970) Slavery and Slave Revolts: A Socio-Historical Analysis of the first maroon ... *Social and Economic Studies*, 19(3) 289-325
- Warren Whatley (2018) The gun-slave hypothesis and the 18th century British slave trade, *Explorations in Economic History*, v67(C) 80-104
- M. Asante (2010, June 5). Henry Louis gates is wrong about African involvement in the slave trade. *New York Times*
- Michael Craton, Garry Greenland (1978) *Searching for the invisible man: Slaves and Plantation Life in Jamaica.* Cambridge: Harvard University Press
- F. N. Ntloedibe (2018) Revisiting modes of enslavement: the role of raiding, kidnapping and wars in the European slave trade, *African Identities*, 16:3, 349-364
- J. T. Lever (1970) Mulatto Influence on the Gold Coast ... Early Nineteenth Century: Jan Nieser of Elmina. *African Historical Studies*. v3(2) 253/261
- Rebecca Shumway (2011) *The Fante and the Transatlantic Slave Trade.* Rochester, NY: University of Rochester Press
- Vincent Carretta (2012) Sessarakoo, William Ansah (b. c. 1730, d. 1770), African visitor to Britain. *Oxford Dictionary of National Biography.* 04.OU
- Ryan Hanley (2015) The Royal Slave: Nobility, Diplomacy and the "African Prince" in Britain, 1748–1752." *Itinerario* 39.2: 329-347
- Angela Sutton (2015) The Seventeenth-Century Slave Trade in the Documents of the English, Dutch, Swedish, Danish and Prussian Royal Slave Trading Companies. *Slavery & Abolition*, v36(3) 445-459
- Rebecca Shumway (2014) Castle Slaves of the Eighteenth-Century Gold Coast (Ghana) *Slavery & Abolition*, 35:1, 84-98
- Pieter De Marees (1987) *Historical Account of the Gold Coast (1602).* Translated and edited by Albert Van Dantzig and Adam Jones. London
- Pernille Ipsen (2013) The Christened Mulatresses: Euro-African Families in a Slave-Trading Town. *The William and Mary Quarterly,* 70(2) 371-398
- Natalie Everts (2012) Incorporating ...Euro African identity in eighteenth century Elmina: *Transactions of the Historical Society of Ghana,* 14/79–104
- Trevor R. Getz (2003) Mechanisms of slave acquisition and exchange in late eighteenth century Anomabu: *African economic history*, (31) 75-89
- Richard S Dunn, Gary Nash (1972) Jamaica and Slaves Chapters. In *Sugar and Slaves: The Rise of the Planter Class in the English West Indies, 1624-1713*, 149-87. Chapel Hill; London: University of North Carolina Press
- Carla Pestana (2005) English Character and the Fiasco of the Western Design. *Early American Studies*, v3(1) 1–31
- Kenneth Bilby (2006) *True-Born Maroons* (Gainesville, Fl)

Chapter 5

- Robin Blackburn (1977) *The Making of New World Slavery* (London: Verso) 255
- James Walvin (2000) *Britain's Slave Empire.* Tempus Pub Limited
- 'Richard Heming of London', *Legacies of British Slave-ownership database,* http://www.depts-live.ucl.ac.uk/lbs/person/view/2146648859 Sidney Blackmore (2018) The wealth of the Beckfords. In Dakers C. (Ed.), *Fonthill Recovered: A Cultural History* (pp. 242-246) London: UCL
- Kenneth Bilby (1992) *Drums of defiance: Maroon music from the earliest free Black communities in Jamaica.* Washington, DC: Smithsonian
- JNHT (2011) *Sites: Historica Districts: Port Royal.* http://jnht.com/site_port_royal.php
- Marcus Rediker (2004) *Villains of All Nations: Atlantic Pirates in the Golden Age.* Boston: Beacon Press.
- Robert Johnson (2018) What to Do about the Irish in the Caribbean? *Caribbean Quarterly*, 64:3-4, 409-433
- Hilary McD. Beckles (1990) "A 'Riotous and Unruly Lot': Irish Indentured Servants and Freemen in the English West Indies, 1644-1713." *The William and Mary Quarterly* 47, no. 4 (1990): 503–22.
- Joseph John Williams (1932) *Whence the "black irish" of Jamaica?.* L. MacVeagh, Dial Press, Incorporated
- Frederick Douglass (5 December 1850) The North Star: *In* Steve Garner (2007) Atlantic Crossing, *Atlantic Studies*, 4:1, 117-132
- JIS Rochelle Williams (6 August 2018) Sligoville – Jamaica's First Free Village. https://jis.gov.jm/sligoville-jamaicas-first-free-village/
- Nadine Hunt (2010) Expanding the frontiers of western Jamaica through minor Atlantic ports in the eighteenth .... *Canadian Journal of History*, 45(3)
- Trevor Burnard (2020) "A Pack Of Knaves": The Royal African Company, the development of the Jamaican plantation economy and the benefits of monopoly, 1672–1708. *Journal of Colonialism and Colonial History*, 21(2)
- Marcus Rediker (2004) *Villains of All Nations: Atlantic Pirates in the Golden Age.* Boston: Beacon Press
- Madeleine Burnside, Rosemarie Robotha (1997) *Spirits of the Passage; The Transatlantic Slave Trade in the Seventeenth Century* (NY: Simon & Schuster)
- Voyages Database.org: www.slavevoyages.org / Slavery Legacies https://www.ucl.ac.uk/lbs/person/view/2146635625
- Tim Armstrong (2004) Slavery, insurance, and sacrifice in the Black Atlantic. *Sea changes: Historicizing the ocean*, 167-8
- James Walvin (2011) *The Zong: A massacre, the law & the end of slavery.* Yale University Press
- Jamaica Gleaner.com (27 December 2020) Kris Manjapra, *The Zong and the ocean's voice.* https://jamaicagleaner.com/article/focus/20201227/kris-manjapra-zong-and-oceans-voice
- Devin Leigh (2020) A Disagreeable Text, *New West Indian Guide / Nieuwe West-Indische Gids*, 94(1-2) 39-74
- Kenneth Morgan (2016). Merchant networks, the guarantee system and the British slave trade to Jamaica in the 1790s. *Slavery & Abolition*, 37(2), 334-352
- David Dabydeen, Hogarth's Blacks: Images of Blacks in Eighteenth Century English Art (Athens, GA: *University of Georgia Press*, 1987);

Chapter 6

- Jorge L. Giovannetti (2006) Grounds of Race, *Latin American and Caribbean Ethnic Studies*, 1:1, 5-36
- *Encyclopedia Britannica* (2020) Audrey Smedley, Peter Wade, Yasuko I. Takezawa, authors. Race. *Encyclopedia Britannica*, inc,
- Richard S Dunn (1972) Sugar and Slaves: The Rise of the Planter Class in the English West Indies, 1624-1713. *Omohundro Institute of Early American History and Culture. University of North Carolina Press*
- UNESCO (2021) Healing the wounds of the slave trade and slavery. Approaches and Practices: a Desk Review. Guerrand-Hermes Foundation for Peace.
- University of Pennsylvania (4 October 2018) A new take on the 19th-century skull collection of Samuels Morton. *ScienceDaily.*
- Charles A Gallagher (2007) White. In *Handbook of the Sociology of Racial and Ethnic Relations.* Ed: Hernan Vera and Joe R. Feagin. New York: Springer 9–14.
- Benjamin Braude (2011) Curse of Ham in the Early Modern Era: The Bible and the Justifications for Slavery. *The Catholic Historical Review* 97.3:587-588
- David M Goldenberg (2009) *The curse of Ham.* Princeton University Press
- *New World Encyclopedia*: Curse of Ham by Simona Brkic (11 May 2020). *New World Encyclopedia.*
- Dean A. Miller (2005) *The Curse of Ham. Race and Slavery in Early Judaism, Christianity, and Islam.* By David M. Goldenberg (2005) (Princeton/Oxford: Princeton University Press, (2003), *Journal of Social History*, v(38)3, 831–833
- Anders Bergström, Chris Stringer et al (2021) Origins of modern human ancestry. *Nature* 590, 229–237
- Natural History Museum, Kerry Lotzof (no date) Human Evolution: Cheddar Man, Mesolithic Britain's blue-eyed boy. https://www.nhm.ac.uk/
- Orlando Patterson (1973) *The Sociology of Slavery* (London)
- E. T. Thompson (1975) Plantation Societies, Race Relations, and the South: *The Regimentation of Population, Selected Papers of Edgar T. Thompson,* DUP

Chapter 6 continued

- Michel-Rolph Trouillot (1998) Culture on the edges: creolization in the plantation context: *Plantation Society in the Americas* v5(1) 8–28
- James A Delle (2009) The Governor and the Enslaved: An Archaeology of Colonial Modernity at Marshall's Pen, Jamaica. *International Journal of Historical Archaeology*, v13(4) 488–512
- Arnold Sio (1976) Race, Colour, and Miscegenation: The Free Coloured of Jamaica and Barbados. *Caribbean Studies*, 16(1) 5-21
- Michael Craton (1997) *Empire, enslavement, and freedom in the Caribbean.* Markus Wiener Pub.
- Tekla Ali Johnson (2004) "The enduring function of caste: colonial and modern Haiti, Jamaica, and Brazil The economy of race, the social organization of caste, and the formulation of racial societies." *Comparative American Studies An International Journal* 2.1 (2004): 61-73.
- Christopher A Charles (2011) Skin bleaching and the prestige complexion of sexual attraction. *Sexuality & Culture*, 15(4) 375-390
- David B Ryden (2018) Manumission in Late Eighteenth-Century Jamaica, *New West Indian Guide* 92(3-4) 211-244
- Adam Rutherford (16 March 2020) How to Argue with a racist: Five myths debunked:. Science & Environment: BBC News *https://www.bbc.co.uk/news/science-environment-51914782*
- Stephen Small (1994) Racial group boundaries and identities: People of 'mixed-race' in slavery across the Americas. *Slavery and Abolition*, 15(3), 17-37.
- Maria Alessandra Bollettino, et al (2020) All spirited likely young lads': free men of colour, the defence of Jamaica, and subjecthood during the American War for Independence, *Slavery & Abolition*, 41:2, 187 211
- Christopher Tomlins (2009) Transplants and timing: Passages in the creation of an Anglo-American law of slavery. *Theoretical Inquiries in Law*, 10(2) 389-421

Chapter 7

- Pieter Spierenburg (1984) The Spectacle of Suffering: Executions and the Evolution of Repression. *Cambridge*, 1984.
- Diane Paton (2001). Punishment, Crime, and the Bodies of Slaves in Eighteenth-Century Jamaica. *Journal of Social History* 34(4) 923-954
- UNESCO (2021) Healing the Wounds of Slave Trade and Slavery. The UNESCO Slave Route Project / GHFP Research Institute
- Robert W. Smith (1945) The Legal Status of Jamaican Slaves Before the Anti-Slavery Movement. *The Journal of Negro History*, 30(3)
- Gale L Kenny (2010) Contentious Liberties: American Abolitionists in Post- Emancipation Jamaica, 1834-1866. Athens, GA: University of Georgia Press.
- Jorge L. Giovannetti (2006) *Grounds of Race, Latin American and Caribbean Ethnic Studies*, 1:1, 5-36
- Michael Craton, James Walvin (1970). *A Jamaican Plantation: The History of Worthy Park 1670-1970.* University of Toronto Press
- Katherine Johnston (2020) Endangered Plantations: Environmental Change and Slavery in the British Caribbean, 1631–1807. *Early American Studies: An Interdisciplinary Journal* 18(3), 259-286
- 'Mona Estate [Jamaica (St Andrew)', *Legacies of British Slave-ownership database, http://wwwdepts-live.ucl.ac.uk/lbs/estate/view/2595*
- 'Jamaica Hanover 138 (Georgia Estate)', *Legacies of British Slave-ownership database, http://wwwdepts-live.ucl.ac.uk/lbs/claim/view/14955*
- 'Jamaica Hanover 139 (Dundee Pen)', *Legacies of British Slave-ownership database, http://wwwdepts-live.ucl.ac.uk/lbs/claim/view/14956*
- Franklin W Knight (1992b) MA 'Introduction' in Slave and Citizen, ed. F. Tannenbaum, *Beacon Press*, Boston, v–xiv.
- Michael Craton et al (1978) Searching for the invisible man: Slaves and Plantation Life in Jamaica. *Cambridge*: Harvard University Press
- S Smith, et al (2006) Requisites of a Considerable Trade: The Letters of Robert, …, 1752-58. *The English Historical Review*, 124(508) 545-570
- Hilary McD Beckles (2019) Running in Jamaica: A Slavery Ecosystem. *The William and Mary Quarterly*, v76(1) 9-14
- 'Charles Knight', Legacies of British Slave-ownership database, http://wwwdepts-live.ucl.ac.uk/lbs/person/view/2146653247
- James Walvin (2007) *A short history of slavery.* Penguin UK
- William Sayers (2007) The Old English Antecedents of *ferry* and *wherry*, ANQ: *A Quarterly Journal of Short Articles, Notes and Reviews*, 20:2, 3-8
- Trevor Burnard, Kenneth Morgan (2001) The dynamics of the slave market and slave purchasing patterns in Jamaica, 1655-1788. *William Mary Q* 58(1):205-28.
- Barry W. Higman (2005*) Plantation Jamaica 1750-1850 Capital and Control in …* 41-93
- Barry W. Higman (2012) Eight Iterations of Lady Nugent's Jamaica Journal." *Kunapipi* 34.2:20
- Hilary Beckles (2007) The Wilberforce Song: How Enslaved Caribbean Blacks Heard British Abolitionists. *Parliamentary History*, v26(S1) 113
- Thomas Holt (1992) *The Problem of Freedom: Race, Labor, and Politics in Jamaica and Britain, 1832–1938.* Baltimore: Johns Hopkins University Press.
- Don McGlashan, et al (2008) *Jamaica: Country Report to the FAO International Technical Conference on Plant Genetic Resources for Food and Agriculture.* FAO The Second Report on the State of the World's Plant Genetic Resources.

Chapter 8

- Beth Fowkes Tobin (1999) *Picturing Imperial Power Colonial Subjects in Eighteenth-century British Painting.* Duke University Press
- James Robertson (2008) Late Seventeenth-Century Spanish Town, Jamaica: Building an English City on Spanish Foundations. *Early American Studies: An Interdisciplinary Journal*, 6, 346 - 390.
- Sandra W Meditz, Dennis M. Hanratty, Library of Congress (1989) *Islands of the Commonwealth Caribbean: ….* Washington, D.C. Federal Research
- Julius S Scott (1986) *The Common Wind: Currents of Afro-American Communication in the Era of the Haitian Revolution (Caribbean).* Diss. Duke University
- Laura M Smalligan, (2011) An Effigy for the Enslaved: Jonkonnu in Jamaica and Belisario's Sketches of Character. *Slavery & Abolition*, v 32(4) 561-581.
- Kenneth Bilby (2010) Surviving Secularization: Masking the Spirit in the Jankunu … Festivals of the Caribbean, *Nieuwe West-Indische Gids*, 84(3,4) 179-223
- Dianne Stewart (2005) *Three Eyes for the Journey: African Dimensions of the Jamaican Religious Experience.* Oxford: Oxford University Press.
- W.T. Lhamon Jr (1998) Raising Cain: Blackface Performance from Jim Crow to Hip Hop. Harvard University Press (Cambridge, MA)
- Nicole Aljoe. Elizabeth Dillon (2017) Conclusion: Jaw Bone or House John Canoe and Koo-Koo Actor Boy in 1837/1838 Caribbean Carnival Exhibit: An Act of Opposition. *The Early Caribbean Digital Archive.* Northeastern University. ecda.northeastern.edu
- Orlando Patterson (1970) A Socio-Historical Analysis of the first maroon war Jamaica 1655 – 1740. *Social and Economic Studies*, 19(3), 289-325
- Simon Newman (2018) Hidden in plain sight: Long-term escaped slaves in late-eighteenth and early-nineteenth century Jamaica. *William and Mary Quarterly*
- Hilary McD Beckles (2019) Running in Jamaica: A Slavery Ecosystem. *The William and Mary Quarterly*, v76(1) 9-14
- Douglas B Chambers (2013) Jamaica Runaway Slaves: 18th and 19th Centuries: *Documenting Runaway Slaves*
- Michael Mullin (1985) Women, and the comparative study of American Negro slavery. *Slavery and Abolition*, 6:1, 25-40
- Laurent Dubois (2008) On the History of the Jamaican Maroons [Review of *True-Born Maroons*, by K. Bilby]. *The Journal of African American History*, 93(1)64-69
- H.A. Murdoch (2009) A Legacy of Trauma: Caribbean Slavery, Race, Class, and Contemporary Identity in Abeng". *Research in African Literatures*, 65-88.
- Encyclopedia Britannica. Pamela D Reed, (30 Jun 2017) Maroon community. *Encyclopedia Britannica*
- SAGE. S McDougal (2009) Nanny. In M. K. Asante, & A. Mazama (Eds.), *Encyclopedia of African religion* (441-442) SAGE Publications, Inc.

Chapter 9

- Vincent Brown (2020) *Tacky's Revolt: the story of an Atlantic Slave War*. Cambridge, Mass.: Harvard University Press
- Clinton Hutton (June 17 2015) Paul Bogle: A Leader in the struggle for the re-definition of post-slavery society. *The Jamaica-Gleaner.com*
- Vincent Brown (2012) Slave Revolt in Jamaica 1760-1761 A Cartographic Narrative. http://revolt.axismaps.com/project.html Interactive map
- Eric Williams (1994) Capitalism and Slavery. 1944. *Chapel Hill: University of North Carolina Press*
- Seymour Drescher (2012) The Shocking Birth of British Abolitionism, *Slavery & Abolition*, 33:4, 571-593
- Pernille Røge (2014) "Why the danes got there first–A trans-imperial study of the abolition of the danish slave trade in 1792." *Slavery & Abolition* 35.4
- Mary Reckord (1968) The Jamaica Slave Rebellion of 1831 *Past & Present*, no. 40, 1968, pp. 108-125.
- David Geggus (2014) Slave rebellion during the Age of Revolution. In *Curaçao in the Age of Revolutions, 1795-1800* (pp. 23-56). Brill.
- Wim Klooster (2014) Slave Revolts, Royal Justice, and a Ubiquitous Rumour in the Age of Revolutions. *The William and Mary Quarterly*, 71(3) 401-424
- Mary Reckord (1971) IV. The Colonial Office and the Abolition of Slavery. *The Historical Journal*, 14(4), 723-734
- *Kingston Gleaner* (March 11 1939) Jamaica's First Sit Down Strike. Kingston, JM. p.25. https://newspaperarchive.com/kingston-gleaner-mar-11-1939-p-25/
- David Geggus (2011) Slave rebellion during the Age of Revolution. In W Klooster et al G. (Eds.), *Curaçao in the Age of Revolutions, 1795-1800*. 23-56.
- *Nottingham Review* and General Advertiser for the Midland Counties (7 April 1832) *Negro Slavery*. Northamptonshire, England
- James Lockett (1999) The Deportation of the Maroons of Trelawny Town to Nova Scotia, Then Back to Africa. *Journal of Black Studies*, v30(1) 5–14
- The Old Gleaner by Rebecca Tortello *A Jamaica Gleaner Feature* (2001) and 2003 *https://old.jamaica-gleaner.com/pages/history/story006.html*
- Christopher Bischof, (2016) Chinese Labourers, Free Blacks, and Social Engineering in the Post-Emancipation British …, *Past & Present*, v2311) 129–168
- Lorna Simmonds (1984) Civil Disturbances in Western Jamaica, 1838-1865. *Jamaican Historical Review*, 14, 1
- Devin Leigh (2020) A Disagreeable Text, New West Indian Guide / *Nieuwe West-Indische Gids*, 94(1-2) 39-74
- Gad Heuman (1994) The Killing Time: The Morant Bay Rebellion in Jamaica. *MacMillan Caribbean*
- Mukhtar Ali Isani (1997) Far from "Gambia's Golden Shore": The Black in Late Eighteenth-Century …. *The William and Mary Quarterly*, 3rd ser., 36 (3): 353)
- Jamaicans.com (no date) Jacob DeCordova, the Jewish Jamaican who founded the Jamaican *Daily Gleaner newspaper*, by Pauline Ford-Caesar.
- Stanley Mirvis (2020) The Jews of Eighteenth-Century Jamaica: New Haven, CT: Yale University Press. 285 CT: YUP. *AJS Review*, v45(1) 86

Chapter 10

- Mariella Scerri (2020) Is Mary Seacole the new mother of nursing? Hektoen International Journal: *Hektoen Institute of Medicine*
- Evelyn J Hawthorne (2000) Self-writing, literary traditions, and post-emancipation identity: the case of Mary Seacole. *Biography*: 309-331
- Razak Gyasi et al (2015) Prevalence and pattern of traditional medical therapy utilisation in Kumasi … Ghana. *Journal of Ethnopharmacology, 161*, 138-146
- Amy Robinson (1994) Authority and the Public Display …: Wonderful Adventures of Mrs. Seacole in Many Lands. *Feminist Studies*, 20(3), 537-557
- Sandra Paquet (2017) The Enigma of Arrival: The Wonderful Adventures of Mrs. Seacole in Many Lands. *African American Review*, v50(4) 864-876
- Lorraine Mercer (2005) I Shall Make No Excuse: The Narrative Odyssey of Mary Seacole." *Journal of Narrative Theory*, v35(1) 1-24. Project MUSE
- Kingston Gleaner, (10 November 2021) Pg. 4, Kingston, Kingston, JM. https://newspaperarchive.com/kingston-gleaner-nov-10-2021-p-4/
- Charles Price (2003) *Cleave to the Black: expressions of Ethiopianism in Jamaica*. NWIG. 77.
- Jamaica Gleaner (2 August 2015, Paul H Williams) *Vindicate Bedward now! MP, August Town residents want end to myth of lunacy*. Jamaica-gleaner.com
- J.M. Washington (1980) *Black Apostles: Afro-American Clergy Confront the Twentieth Century*. Ed. R. Burkett and R. Newman. Boston, GK Hall & Co.
- A.A. Brooks (1917) *History of Bedwardism, Or, The Jamaica Native Baptist Free Church, Union Camp, Augustown, St. Andrew, Ja., BWI.* Gleaner Company
- David Gosse (18 May 2021) The Arrest of Bedward and its Socio-Cultural Legacies. UWI. *Jamaica National Heritage Trust*. https://youtu.be/jnoc93i8iyQ
- Simboonath Singh (2004) Resistance …A comparison of the Back to Africa, Black Power, and Rastafari movements. *Journal of African American Studies* 8(3)18-36
- Ramla Bandele (2010) Understanding African diaspora political activism: the rise and fall of the Black Star Line. *Journal of black studies*, 40(4), 745-761
- Rupert Lewis (24 April 1997) Marcus Garvey and racism. Letters. *Kingston Gleaner*, p5 https://newspaperarchive.com/kingston-gleaner-apr-24-1997-p-5/Rev George McGuire. In. John L Graves (1962) The social ideas of Marcus Garvey. *The Journal of Negro Education* 31.1: 65-74/
- Adam Ewing (2011) Garvey or Garveyism? *Transition* 105:130-4
- Richard A Howard (1953) *Captain Bligh and the Breadfruit. Scientific American*, 1v88(3) 88–95
- Jamaican Information Service (n.d.) *Jamaican National Symbols. Symbols and Emblems*. https://nlj.gov.jm/jamaican-national-symbols
- Peter Pellizzari (2020) Supplying slavery: Jamaica, North America, and British intra-imperial trade, 1752–1769, *Slavery & Abolition*, v41(3) 528-554
- John Rashford (2001) Those that do Not Smile Will Kill Me: The Ethnobotany of the Ackee in Jamaica. *Economic Botany*, v55(2) 190-211The Sunday Gleaner (27/04/2014) Anthony Gambrill. Read cook nyam Newspaper Archives newspaperarchive.com/kingston-gleaner-apr-27-2014-p-70/
- Caitlyn Hitt (2018) Jamie Oliver's net worth revealed after chef is slammed over Jerk rice product. *Daily Mail Online*
- Delano Franklyn (2010) Sport in Jamaica: A Local and International Perspective. *GraceKennedy Foundation*
- Sasha Turner (2016) Race Pride, National Identity, and Jamaican Athletics. *Black Perspectives*: AAIHS.org
- Robert Trivers et al JT (2013) The Symmetry of Children's Knees Is Linked to Their Adult Sprinting Speed and Their Willingness to Sprint in a Long-Term Jamaican Study. *PLOS ONE* 8(8): e72244
- Nazma Muller (July/August 2012) Why do Jamaicans run so fast? *Caribbean Beat*. MEP Publishers.

Chapter 11

- William Aiken (2006) The Athletic Prowess of Jamaicans In: Orville W. Taylor (2015) It's Culture, Not Genes: Explaining Why Jamaican Sprinters Are the Fastest Humans on Earth, *Caribbean Quarterly*, 61:1, 23-41
- Orville W. Taylor (2015) It's Culture, Not Genes: Why Jamaican Sprinters Are the Fastest Humans on Earth, *Caribbean Quarterly*, 61:1, 23-41
- SAGE (2012) *Encyclopedia of Global Religion: Jamaica*. SAGE Publications. Edited by Mark Juergensmeyer & Wade Clark Roo
- Erin Mackie (2005) Welcome the outlaw: pirates, maroons, and Caribbean countercultures. *Cultural Critique* 59:24-62
- The Daily Gleaner (29 August 1934) "Police of Kingston and the Purveyors of a Religious Cult," *The Daily Gleaner*, p 7.
- Monique A Bedasse (2021) Rastafari, the Transnational Archive, and Postcolonial Caribbean Intellectual History. *Small Axe: A Caribbean Journal of Criticism*, 25(1), 116-131
- K.P. Naphtali (1999) *The testimony of His Imperial Majesty Emperor Haile Selassie I: Defender of the Christian faith*. Washington, DC: Zewd
- Mento music: *https://jamaica55.gov.jm/in-a-nutshell-jamaica/jamaica%E2%80%99s-heritage-in-dance-and-music/*
- Stephen Foehr (2000) *Jamaican Warriors: Reggae, Roots & Culture*. Sanctuary Pub Limited
- Jamaica Gleaner (15 October 2006) Millie not so 'small' anymore. *The Gleaner*. http://old.jamaica-gleaner.com/gleaner/20061015/ent/ent4.html

Chapter 11 continued

- (NLJ Biographies) *National Library of Jamaica. Millicent Small (1946-2020) https://nlj.gov.jm/project/millicent-small-1946/*
- SAGE (2019) Ska. *The SAGE International Encyclopedia of Music and Culture.* SAGE Publications. Janet Sturman, editor
- Paul Kauppila (2006) From Memphis to Kingston: An Investigation into the Origin of Jamaican Ska: *Social and Economic Studies,* v55(1/2) UWI 75–91
- Khytie K. Brown (2018) The Spirit of Dancehall: embodying a new nomos in Jamaica. *Transition, 125,* 17–31. https://doi.org/10.2979/transition.125.1.04
- Norman Stolzoff (2002) Wake the town and tell the people: Dancehall culture in Jamaica. *Journal of Popular Music Studies, 14*(2), 166-167.
- Jérémie Kroubo Dagnini (2018) Kingston: A Societal Patchwork. *Études caribéennes* 39-40
- Jérémie Kroubo Dagnini (2011) The importance of reggae music in the worldwide cultural universe. *Études caribéennes* 16
- Colin G. Clarke (1966) Population pressure in Kingston, Jamaica: ... *Transactions of the Institute of British Geographers,* 38(1)165–182
- John Vilanova (2019) Kingston Be Wise: Jamaica's Reggae Revival, Musical Livity, and Troubling ... *International Journal of Communication* 13:20
- Christopher Whyms-Stone (2005) *Urban Case Study. The Government Yards of Trench Town*: Conference for the Built Environment, Kingston, Jamaica
- Kevon Rhiney and Romain Cruse (2012) Trench Town Rock: Reggae Music, Landscape Inscription, ... in Kingston, Jamaica. *Urban Studies Research*
- Library of Congress tunes in to *'The Harder They Come'* (24 March 2021) by Yasmine Peru. https://jamaica-gleaner.com/article/entertainment/20210324/library-congress-tunes-harder-they-come
- Gail Ferguson et al (2006) Get Up, Stand Up, Stand Up for Your Rights!' The Jamaicanisation of Youth Across 11 Countries Through Reggae Music?" *Journal of Cross-Cultural Psychology,* v47(4) 581–604
- Molefi Kete Asante et al (2005) Reggae: *Encyclopedia of Black Studies.* SAGE Publications, Inc. City: Thousand Oaks: 413-414
- John Aarons (1999) National Cultural Policy of Jamaica Executive Director, Recording Industry Association of America. *National Library of Jamaica*
- Anya Zilberstein (2016) Bastard Breadfruit and Other Cheap Provisions: Early Food Science for the .... *Early Science and Medicine,* v21(5) 492–508
- Andrew David (1993) 4. Bligh's Successful Breadfruit Voyage. *RSA Journal,* v141(5444) 821–824
- Richard A Howard (1953) Captain Bligh and the Breadfruit. *Scientific American,* 1v88(3) 88–95
- Debbian Wray, et al (2020) Ackee (Blighia Sapida KD Koenig)-A Review of Its Economic Importance, Bioactive Components, Associated Health Benefits and Commercial Applications. *International Journal of Fruit Science,* 20(sup2), S910-S924.
- Peter Pellizzari (2020) Supplying slavery: Jamaica, North America, and British intra-imperial trade, 1752–1769, *Slavery & Abolition,* v41(3) 528-554
- John Rashford (2001) Those that do Not Smile Will Kill Me: The Ethnobotany of the Ackee in Jamaica. *Economic Botany,* v55(2) 190-211
- The Sunday Gleaner (27/04/2014) Anthony Gambrill. Read cook nyam *Newspaper Archives* newspaperarchive.com/kingston-gleaner-apr-27-2014-p-70/
- Caitlyn Hitt (2018) Jamie Oliver's net worth revealed after chef is slammed over Jerk rice product. *Daily Mail Online*
- Delano Franklyn (2010) *Sport in Jamaica: A Local and International Perspective.* GraceKennedy Foundation
- Sasha Turner (2016) Race Pride, National Identity, and Jamaican Athletics. *Black Perspectives*: AAIHS.org
- Robert Trivers et al JT (2013) The Symmetry of Children's Knees Is Linked to Their Adult Sprinting Speed and Their Willingness to Sprint in a Long-Term Jamaican Study. *PLOS ONE* 8(8): e72244

Chapter 12

- Nazma Muller (July/August 2012) Why do Jamaicans run so fast? *Caribbean Beat.* MEP Publishers
- Dictionary.com *https://www.dictionary.com/browse/reparation;* Merriam-Webster.com Dictionary, *Reparation. https://www.merriam-webster.com/dictionary/reparation*
- Professors Luke Moffett, Katarina Schwarz (2018) Reparations for the Transatlantic Slave Trade and Historical Enslavement: Linking past atrocities with contemporary victim populations. *Netherlands Quarterly of Human Rights.* 36(4) 247-269
- Sir Hilary Beckles (2014) Chairman of CARICOM Reparations Commission Addresses British House of Commons. *CARICOM Press Release* 188/2014
- Dorbrene E O'Marde (2014) Reparations: An Opportunity for Direct Foreign Investment in the Region: *Social and Economic Studies* 69.1/2: 243A-249A
- Allan D Cooper (2012) From Slavery to Genocide: The Fallacy of Debt in Reparations Discourse. *Journal of Black Studies,* 43(2) 107–126
- Claudia Rauhut (2018) Mobilizing Transnational Agency for Slavery Reparations. .... Jamaica. *The Journal of African American History* 103.12 133-162
- Hugh Paget (1945) The free village system in Jamaica. Jamaican Historical Review, 1(1), 31
- Thomas McCarthy (2004). Coming to terms with our past, Part II: On the morality and politics of reparations for slavery. *Political Theory,* 32(6)750-772
- John Richard Oldfield (2012) Repairing historical wrongs: Public history and transatlantic slavery. *Social & Legal Studies* 21(2) 243-255
- Giulia Bonacci (2020) They Took Us by Boat and We're Coming Back by Plane. An Assessment of Rastafari and Repatriation. IDEAZ, *Department of Sociology, University of the West Indies,* 15:150-165. ffhal-03326193
- Michael Barnett (2019) Rastafari Repatriation as Part of the Caribbean Reparations Movement. *Social and Economic Studies,* v68(3-4) 61-263
- Giulia Bonacci (2020) They Took Us by Boat and We're Coming Back by Plane. An Assessment of Rastafari and Repatriation. IDEAZ, *Department of Sociology, University of the West Indies,* 15:150-165. ffhal-03326193

Scroll Quotes (primary sources)

			PAGES
1	34	Sir Hans Sloane (1707–25) *A Voyage to the Islands of Madera, Barbados, Nevis, S. Christophers and Jamaica*, 2 Vols. (British Museum), vI, lvii	5,69
2		Patrick Browne (1756) *The Civil and Natural History of Jamaica*, London	7
3		John Gifford (1894) The Karifs and Insular Caribs. *Science 23*, 573:45-46	10
4		James Henry Collens (1896) *Centenary of Trinidad*, 1797-1897. Port of Spain, Trinidad: Government Printing Office	11
5		Translated from Cristóbal Colón's voyages by Andres Bernaldez, (1930) *Historia de los Reyes Catholics. The Voyages of Christopher Columbus, Being the Journals of his First and Third, and the Letters* … Notes by Cecil Jane	12
6		Juan Fernández de Angulo, in 1540 in Sermon of Fray Antonio Montesinos. Santo Domingo, 1511	15
		El sermon of Fray Antonio de Montesinos, 1511. https://www.colonialzone-dr.com/montecino/	
7		Gonzalo Fernandez de Ovideo y Valdes: 1535. (1535) Historia General de las Indias. *Libros* 1-20. Sevilla.	17
8 9		Bartolomé de Las Casas 1542. *A Short Account of the Destruction of the Indies*. Trans. Nigel Griffin. New York: Penguin Books (1999).	18
10		*A collection of treaties of peace and commerce* (1714) printed for J. Baker at the Black Boy in Pater-Noster-Row London: J. Baker.	19
11	30	James Mursell Phillippo (1843) *Jamaica: Its Past and Present State*. United Kingdom, J. Snow	21,60
12		Peter Thomson, editor (2009) Henry Drax's Instructions on the Management of a Seventeenth Century Barbadian Sugar Plantation. 1679, *William and Mary Quarterly*, third series. 66 585-604	22
13		Venatius Chukwudum Oforka (2015) *The Bleeding Continent*: How Africa Became Impoverished and Why It Remains Poor (Xlibris Corporation) 97	27
14		Thomas Bowdich (1819) *Mission from Cape Coast Castle to Ashantee*. London: John Murray p.274-275	28
15		Anthony Benezet (1784) *The Case of Our Fellow-creatures*: The Oppressed Africans, Respectfully Recommended to the Serious Consideration of the Legislature of Great-Britain, by the People Called Quakers v8. James Phillips	30
16		Richard Thelwall, Annamaboe, (28 September 1682) in The English in West Africa 1681–1683: The Local Correspondence of the Royal African Company of England 1681-1699, edited. Robin Law, 119–20	30
17	18 19	William Hutton (1821) *A Voyage to Africa*: Including a Narrative of an Embassy to One of the Interior Kingdoms	31,32
20		[Gregory Butler] to General Disbrowe [1655] State Papers of John Thurloe, 3: 689 *In* Carla Gardina Pestana (2005) English Character and the Fiasco of the Western Design. *Early American Studies*, v3(1) 1–31	37
21		Indenture Agreement Patrick Burke, 1739, London; *The Jamaican Family Search Genealogy Research Library*.	40
22		Granville Sharp's Letter re Zong incident 23 May 1783 (*Gloucestershire Archives D3549 13/1/B1*)	42
23		Alexander Falconbridge (1788), *An Account of the Slave Trade on the Coast of Africa* (London) repr. New York,17	43
24		Elizabeth Donnan 1883-1955, editor *Documents illustrative of the history of the slave trade to America* [by] Elizabeth Donnan (v4) 131	46
25		Acts of Assembly passed in the Island of Jamaica from the year 1681 to the year 1769 inclusive. In Two Volumes. Vol. II Saint Jago De La Vega. Jamaica. Printed by Lowry and Sherlock. https://archive.org/details/actsofassemblypa02jama/page/n6/mode/2up?q=Jack p 92	48
26		W. J. Gardner (1873) *A history of Jamaica from its discovery by Christopher Columbus to the present time*: including an account of its trade and agriculture; sketches of the manners, habits, and customs of all classes of its inhabitants; and a narrative of the progress of religion and education in the island. London: E. Stock. https://babel.hathitrust.org/cgi/pt?id=hvd.32044011833951&view=1up&seq=16	51
27		William Beckford (1788) *Remarks Upon the Situation of Negroes in Jamaica: Impartially Made from a Local Experience of Nearly Thirteen Years in that Island*. T. and J. Egerton p.33	53
28		Queen Elizabeth. Acts of the Privy Council of England Volume 26, 1596-1597.John Roche Dasent. London: His Majesty's Stationery Office, 1902. 1-25. *British History Online*. https://www.british-history.ac.uk/acts-privy-council/vol26/pp1-25 (p16)	59
29		"Cecil Papers: December 1601, 26-31." *Calendar of the Cecil Papers in Hatfield House*: Volume 11, 1601. Ed. R A Roberts. London: His Majesty's Stationery Office, 1906. 531-588. British History Online. http://www.british-history.ac.uk/cal-cecil-papers/vol11/pp531-588 Endorsed. "Minute, 1601." 1¼ pp. (**91.** 15.)	59
31		Lieutenant Governor, Phillip Thicknesse 1719-1792. *Memoirs And Anecdotes of Philip Thicknesse*: Late Lieutenant Governor of Land Guard Fort, And Unfortunately Father to George Touchet, Baron Audley. Dublin: Printed by Graisberry and Campbell for William Jones, 1790. 96(p74)	64
32		'Zachary Bayly', Legacies of British Slavery database. http://wwwdepts-live.ucl.ac.uk/lbs/person/view/2146652013	65
33		British Imperial Act 1833. Courtesy of Parliamentary Archives. Ministry of Government and Consumer Services. *Archives of Ontario*. http://www.archives.gov.on.ca/en/explore/online/black_history/big/big_02_imperial_act.aspx	69
35		Ignatius Sancho Ignatius (1784) *Letters of the Late Ignatius Sancho*, An African: To Which Are Prefixed. Memoirs of his Life by Joseph Jekyll. 15-367	74
36		Ottobah Cugoano (1787) *Thoughts and Sentiments* on the Evil and Wicked Traffic of the Slavery and Commerce of the Human Species	74
37		Phillip Henry Gosse & Richard Hill (1851) *A Naturalist's Sojourn in Jamaica*. Longman, Brown, Green and Longmans	85

Primary Sources

p.7, 60 Edward Long (1774) *The History of Jamaica or General Survey of the Ancient and Modern State of the Island:* with reflections on its situation settlements, inhabitants, climate, products, commerce, laws and government. 3 vols. (London: T. Lownudes), 731 and 857

p.16 Cristóbal Colón '... fairest isle...' quote 1494. *In* Dr Barry Floyd, (1981) *Jamaica: An Island Microcosm*

p.19 Bristol ships: 'A List of Ships Employ'd in the Trade to Africa from the Port of Bristol the year 1749', CO 388, 45, fols 5–6. *The National Archives*, Kew.

p.25 Ottobah Cugoano (1787) *Thoughts and Sentiments on the Evil and Wicked Traffic of the Slavery and Commerce of the Human Species*

p.28 William Sherwood evidence, Dec. 3, 1789, *Journals of the Assembly of Jamaica*, 8 (March-October 19, 1784)

p.28 House of Commons Sessional Papers, 68:154, 165; Simon Taylor to Robert Taylor, Holland, Jamaica, May 10, 1806, Simon Taylor Letter Book, *Institute of Commonwealth Studies Library, University of London*

p.30 John Newton (1788) *Thoughts upon the Atlantic slave trade*. London: J. Buckland and J. Johnson

p.33 No Author (1749) *The Royal African: or, Memoirs of the Young Prince of Annamaboe:*(London: W. Reeve)

p.34 Capt. William Taylor with Rich'd Brew & Co., Account record by Richard Brew in Annamaboe [Anomabu, Ghana] for Captain William Taylor. Oct. 26, 1710.Slavery Collection, *New York Historical Society*, nyhs_sc_b-02_f-18_002.

Bill of sale for "six Negro slaves…Cato, William, Trouble, Quaco, Jannette, & Holly [Molly?]," purchased by Mr. John Joyce of Kingston [Jamaica] from Henry J. Kerreth. *New York Historical Society*

p.35 Account record for the sale of 75 slaves from the cargo of the Brig Othello, sold by Francis Mairez and David Cooper of Montego Bay, Jamaica, on behalf of Samuel and William Vernon [of Newport, Rhode Island]. *New York Historical Society*. https://digitalcollections.nyhistory.org/islandora/object/islandora%3A142634#page/3/mode/

p.31,37,41,48 52,62-64 Bryan Edwards (1798) *The History Civil and Commercial of the British Colonies in the West Indies*: To which is Added, an Historical Survey of the French Colony in the Island of St. Domingo (Vol. 44108). B. Crosby.

p.43,53,55 W. J. Gardner (1873) *Sketches of the Manners, Habits, and Customs of all Classes of its Inhabitants*; and a Narrative of the Progress of Religion and Education in the Island

p. 46 Richard Watson (preached 1824) Sermon V: the religious instruction of the slaves in the West India colonies advocated and defended, in *The Works of the Rev. Richard Watson*, 12 vols., London, 1858, ii, 88-97

p.47 Commander Bedford Pim, Royal Navy (1866). *The Negro and Jamaica*. London: Trübner and Co. Paternoster Row: https://babel.hathitrust.org/cgi/pt?id=mdp.39015008194667&view=2up&seq=6&skin=2021

p.48 Anon (1790) *Marly; or, A Planter's Life in Jamaica* (Glasgow)

p.49 National Archives 1831 Ref. CO 137/181 (71) *Slave insurrection, Jamaica*

p.51 Anon (1828) *Marly; or, A Planter's Life in Jamaica* (Glasgow)

p.52 John Broderick (1895 (The Manager of Rose Hall) The Notorious Mrs Palmer. *Kingston Daily Gleaner*, May 10, 1895:7. Newspaper Archives

p.54, 55 Rev. Richard Bickell (1825) *The West Indies as they are; or, a real picture of Slavery: but more particularly as it exists in the island of Jamaica in three parts*. London: J. Hatchard and Sons.

p.55 James Grainger (1764) *The Sugar-cane!: A Poem. In Four Books*. With Notes... R. and J. Dodsley.

p.57 *New York Times*. 1859. "Emancipation in Jamaica: Its Results upon the Present and Future Welfare of the Island." *New York Times*, November 18. ProQuest Historical Newspapers, *New York Times (1851–2003) www.nytimes.com*

p.57 Sir Hans Sloane (1707–25) A Voyage to the Islands of Madera, Barbados, Nevis, S. Christophers and Jamaica, 2 Vols. (British Museum), vI, lvii

p.66 Bath Chronicle January, 22, 1761. *The British Newspaper Archive*. www.britishnewspaperarchive.co.uk

p.55,70 James Hakewill 1778-1843 (1825) *A Picturesque Tour of the Island of Jamaica*. London: Hurst and Robinson

p.56 ' Charles Knight ', Legacies of British Slave-ownership database, http://www.depts-live.ucl.ac.uk/lbs/person/view/2146653247

p.56 Jamaica Mercury and Kingston Weekly Advertiser - *In* Folarin Shyllon (1978) Slave Advertisements in the British West Indies. *Caribbean Studies* 18, no. 3/4 (1978): 175–99

p.61 Benjamin Moseley (1799) *A Treatise on Sugar*. London: G.G. and J. Robinson.175-9

p.61 Anonymous (1745) Letter from Jamaica, Feb. 2, *Gentleman's Magazine* 15(4) 218

p.61 The Royal Gazette (Kingston), vol. 21, no. 51 (December 14–21, 1799), 17

p.62 Bryan Edwards, *The History Civil and Commercial of the British Colonies of the West Indies*, Book IV. "Present Inhabitants," accessed online at https://archive.org/details/historycivilcomm04edwa, 2.

Bryan Edwards (1796) The Proceedings of the Governor and Assembly of Jamaica, in regard to the Maroon Negroes: *Jamaica Assembly*. London John Stockdale, Piccadilly

p.64 Chamber Journal (1897) THE STORY OF THE MAROONS. 1897. *Chambers's journal of popular literature, science and arts, Jan.1854-Nov.1897*, 14(723), 711-715.

p.68,69, 71,85 John Stewart (1832) *Colonial slavery: Defence of the Baptist Missionaries from the charge of inciting the late rebellion in Jamaica* … Saturday, December 15, 1832. Sherwood, Gilbert, & Piper, London

p.70 Robert R Madden (1835) *A Twelve month's Residence in the West Indies: During the Transition from Slavery to Apprenticeship …; of Jamaica and Other Islands* (v2) 300. Carey, Lea and Blanchard

p.71 Untitled item (1866) Freedman: a monthly magazine devoted to the interests of the freed coloured people, *Anti-Slavery Reporter* (9) 229-230

p.75,77 Kingston Daily Gleaner, January 22, 1895 Pg. 3, Kingston, Kingston, JM. https://newspaperarchive.com/kingston-daily-gleaner-jan-22-1895-p-3/

p.72 Edward B. Underhill (1865) *The tragedy of Morant Bay: A narrative of the disturbances in the island of Jamaica in 1865*. London, Alexander.

p.74 Ignatius Sancho (1784) *Letters of the Late Ignatius Sancho, An African*: To Which Are Prefixed. Memoirs of his Life by Joseph Jekyll. 15,367

Ottobah Cugoano (1787) *Thoughts and Sentiments* on the Evil and Wicked Traffic of the Slavery and Commerce of the Human Species

Thomas Clarkson (1786) *An essay on the slavery* and commerce of the human species particularly the African: (London) 197

p.75 "The Maroons". The Morant Bay Rebellion extract, entitled *Kingston Gleaner*, Oct 19, 1865, p. 4, NewspaperArchive: https://newspaperarchive.com/kingston-gleaner-oct-19-1865-p-4/ Jamaican Jews

p.76 Willem Bosman (1703) *A New and Accurate Description of the Coast of Guinea*: London

p.81,85 Matthew "Monk" Lewis (1834) *Journal of a West-India Proprietor*: Kept During a Residence in the Island of Jamaica. London, J. Murray

Image Credits

Glossary

Abolition: official ending of the slave trade

Anthropologist: a person who studies the science of human beings and their cultures

Archaeologist: a person who studies the science of objects that people have left behind

Asiento: a contract to buy enslaved people for Spain

Bauxite: a natural sedimentary rock that is converted into aluminium; considered the star performer of Jamaica's economy.

Blackamore: a name for a Black African in previous centuries. Also called "Moor".

Caboceer: African leader trading the British

Chattel slavery: own and treat people, their children and children's children as property – created by white Europeans

CITES: Convention on International Trade in Endangered Species of Wild Fauna and Flora,

Colony: a country controlled by another more powerful country. Jamaica was controlled by Spain and then Britain

Columbian Exchange: the movement of diseases, ideas, food. crops, animals and peoples from Europe to the "New World".

Conquistador: a 15th to 17th century explorer or soldier for the Iberian Peninsula

Discrimination: unfairly treating people because of their race or colour in organisations or socially

Economic historian: a person who studies how money was used in a country in the past

Encomienda: a Spanish legal system that forced Indians to work and pay the Spanish in goods or money

Enslaved: a slave, of being controlled and dominated and without freedom

Emancipation: legal method of freeing enslaved people

Eurocentric: white point of view that ignores, distorts, lies about aspects of history such as culture, ethnicity, race and people; also spreads lies as facts

British slave trade: three routes form a triangle between Africa, Europe, and Americas in the buying and selling of goods and African peoples. Also called triangular or transatlantic slave trade

Enslavement: being controlled, dominated or forced to work for another without payment

Fallacy: an argument which claims to be factual while in reality it is not.

Genocide: to deliberately kill a group of people because of their race, ethnicity, or religion

Geologist: a person who studies rocks scientifically to find out how the Earth changes over time

Historian: a person who studies the passing of time and the events that happen within that time

Illusion: seeing or hearing something and believing it as a fact when it is not true – similar to a trick

Indentured servant: a contract of their own free will to work for a set number of years in exchange for something, such as accommodation costs

Institutionalised or systemic racism: invisible systems of white privileges inherited by organisations, institutions, occupations and professions

Karst: landscapes feature caves, underground streams and sinkholes on the surface

Kingston: Capital city of Jamaica

Lignum vitae: national flower. Leaves created soap suds. Plants and leaves were used as dyes for fabric.

Lineage: people who all have the same common relative from hundreds of years ago.

Matrilineal : inheritance through the mother or the female line.

Manumission: legally giving freedom to enslaved people

Middle passage: crossing the Atlantic Ocean to and from West Central Africa and the Americas on slaving ships

Misappropriate: dominate groups who take, steal, or use part of another culture as their own without acknowledgement; usually from less dominant groups

Mitochondrial DNA: DNA that is passed from mother to child.

Myth: an old story that has been around so long that most people believe it but existing only in their imagination

Negro: derogatory name for Black people, used in the past

Oroonoko: a play based on a 1688 novel by Aphra Behn about an African nobleman sold into enslavement

Parish: Jamaica is divided into 14 parishes and three counties, named mainly after the British

Patios: Most Jamaicans speak Patois which has West African, English, Spanish influences

Plantation: a large farm growing one specific crop

Prejudice: negative judgement about a group without knowledge of the group

Racism: system of advantage for whites based on skin colour

Racist: a person who believes he or she is better and superior to other races, based on skin colour

Reparation: justice or compensation given by the perpetrators of atrocities to their victims; not necessarily in monetary forms

Resistance: refuse to obey orders

Rebellion or insurrection: people who openly fight against laws, and are usually armed

Scientific racism: using science to justify racism, racial inferiority, or racial superiority.

Scramble Sale: a type of auction to sell enslaved people

Taíno: original peoples of Jamaica called Indians who speak an Arawak language; also called indigenous or natives

Treaty of Tordesillas: a promise between Spain and Portugal not to invade certain countries

White man's burden: racist justification for white conquest which required patience because Africans were 'foolish, evil and childlike'

White man's privilege: natural and unrecognised benefits, rights or power, in society, organisations and industries for being born a white male and a white female

White saviour complex: white peoples' condescending attitude of 'saving or rescuing' Black peoples that only benefits their own emotional and /or career gains.

INDEX

Pamela Gayle was born in South London, England, United Kingdom, from Jamaican parents. Pamela has taught in primary schools for over 25 years, with additional responsibilities as Black History Manager.

Pamela's passion is travelling to sites of Black interest, history, and culture, and learning about the Black history that she was never taught at school. She has indulged her wandering spirit by participating in various teacher exchange schemes in Europe, the USA and The Caribbean.

Pamela still lives in South London with her adult son. She would love a cat, but travels too much to look after one. Cycling, chocolate, reggae, salsa and yoga, are her hobbies, but not at the same time – and not necessarily in that order!

This is Pamela's second book as an independent author. If you liked this book, please consider leaving feedback and suggestions on Amazon.

Best wishes

Pamela Gayle

Image 86: Author. Taken at Roxborough Beach, St. Ann's Bay Jamaica.

The Black History Truth: ARGENTINA is the first book in this series published in 2021.

Lightning Source UK Ltd.
Milton Keynes UK
UKHW050627070722
405516UK00009B/571